Steps to Academic Reading 4

In Context

Jean Zukowski/Faust
Susan S. Johnston
Elizabeth E. Templin

THOMSON ™

HEINLE

Australia • Canada • Mexico • Singapore • Spain • United Kingdom • United States

Steps to Academic Reading 4
In Context
Jean Zukowski/Faust
Susan S. Johnston
Elizabeth E. Templin

Developmental Editor: *Phyllis Dobbins*
Production Editor: *Angela Williams Urquhart*
Marketing Manager: *Katrina Byrd*
Manufacturing Coordinator: *Holly Mason*
Production/Composition: *Real Media Solutions*

Copy Editor: *Dina Forbes, WordPlayers*
Cover Designer: *Bill Brammer Design*
Printer: *Webcom*

Printed in Canada.
 4 5 6 7 8 9 10 06 05 04

For more information contact Heinle, 25 Thomson Place, Boston, Massachusetts 02210 USA, or you can visit our Internet site at http://www.heinle.com

For permission to use material from this text or product, contact us:
Tel   1-800-730-2214
Fax   1-800-730-2215
Web http://www.thomsonrights.com

Library of Congress Control Number: 2001095321
ISBN: 0-03-034002-0

Contents

Preface

The third edition of *Steps to Academic Reading 4, In Context* is an intermediate integrated reading skills text that combines high-interest contemporary topics with the strategies of comprehensive skills practice. The primary focus is on academic and practical vocabulary building so as to build strength in predicting, anticipating meaning and ideas from context clues, and reading critically. Each unit imitates the natural way a student of language learns new concepts and integrates ideas: first an anticipatory set is established through prediction activities, thus activating the student's background knowledge of the topic and preparing the student psychologically for a coherent body of new vocabulary and interrelated topics. Next the student works with the related concepts and vocabulary. Then the student reads a main article, one that encompasses the theme of the unit. Related readings, exercises, and questions to hone skills follow, simulating the respiraling process through which students in native language become familiar with words and concepts.

In response to teachers' suggestions, the authors have crafted a preliminary unit and eight chapters with updated information and new readings and exercises. Each unit contains the following features or strategies:

- Anticipatory activities to prepare learners for each unit topic by asking them to predict themes from their own experience
- Pre-reading exercises to introduce key concepts and content-related terms
- Opinion questions that follow the main article, to stimulate inferencing, critical thinking, and discussion
- A vocabulary journal section to encourage students to record new words and concepts systematically
- Vocabulary and structure exercises to recycle the main ideas and vocabulary
- Reading focus strategies to highlight specific skills development such as skimming and scanning, making inferences, drawing conclusions, paraphrasing, summarizing, using context clues, understanding sequences in a variety of reading environments
- Theme expansion through related readings and exercises
- Integration of information and ideas to help students learn to organize and classify data, discus their ideas and opinions, and write about them
- Timed readings to develop increased reading speed and efficiency

In this edition, each unit begins with a reading of over 1000 words in which all reading skills can be practiced. The critical reading strategy sections have been expanded, and there are new timed readings with multiple-choice questions.

The topics, vocabulary, strategies, structures, and activities have been designed for students of English for academic purposes who are already familiar with the basic structures of the language. The focus words have been carefully selected from common word frequency lists of academic language. Although many of the reading topics in this third edition are new, the essence of the previous editions remains intact: the strong emphasis on vocabulary development, the strengthening and integration of reading skills, and the focus on high-interest and broadly applicable topics.

The reading process as an interaction between the student and the text requires that students use their world knowledge to predict what topics the unit will focus on. The strategies that can make students stronger readers are introduced and reinforced. The target vocabulary of the unit is presented in a context-controlled environment to familiarize the students with key words and concepts. The object is to present the student with a number experiences with a new concept so that the student will begin to use it naturally, learning as every student learns. This process helps students to incorporate the new elements into active vocabulary.

The units have been developed with the purpose of forming logical sets of words, members of the same semantic or thematic domain. The target words are used in the long main article on the general topic and in related articles, in which the concepts are developed and reinforced. The activities that follow each reading focus on specific skills such as skimming and scanning, extracting main ideas, making inferences, giving opinions, determining word meanings from context clues, and understanding sequences. The preliminary unit is included to help students become familiar and comfortable with the strategy approach used in the text. The subsequent units present many opportunities to practice the strategies and integrate these skills.

Although the *Steps to Academic Reading 4, In Context* vocabulary list might seem advanced for the intermediate level, extensive class testing shows the opposite to be true: students expect to encounter content-specific terms and concepts within a reading. Furthermore, these high signature words (words that are closely related to one topic and which are obvious to the language learner) tend to be the most easily learned. Students also feel the pvower of these words as they begin to reach for cognitive academic language proficiency.

The following standards have been applied throughout the text to make readings more accessible:

- **A clear topic sentence and identifiable main idea for each paragraph.**
- **Limits on sentence length** (To help students carry slowly increasing concept loads and to avoid taxing but encourage developing the short-term memory, we have used sentences of twelve to fifteen words average length. Longer sentences do occur, as they must in authentic texts, but they are found with introductory elements, which are set off by commas, and in sentences with marked series elements.)

- **Inclusion of signal words** (Nearly all subordinated clauses are marked with a relative pronoun or that, the word both is used to signal a parallel double construction, *either* and *neither* alert students to choices, transitional devices, and marks of punctuation have been incorporated so that students become aware of the types of signals and devices used to contextualize information.)
- **Respiraling of vocabulary** (Some of the target words are introduced in nonessential contexts, focused on in a Vocabulary in Context activity, and then used repeatedly in readings and exercises. Most new items in a unit are used in subsequent units. The readings build on one another, so that the reading level remains constant for students although the book appears to become more challenging.)

Steps to Academic Reading 4, In Context presents topics of general interest, including information technology, educational frontiers, travel, use of the Internet, sociological information about generations, and matters of global importance like protection from the elements and environmental protection.

This new edition has evolved as a result of the many requests and suggestions from users of previous editions, teachers at more institutions than we can name. Thanks to the good people at Heinle, WordPlayers, Real Media Solutions, and our professional colleagues who have worked with us and given us help, solid suggestions, and sound advice.

JZ/F
SSJ
EET

Introduction:
How to Use This Text

Steps to Academic Reading 4, In Context is a book of content lessons for the development and integration of reading and study skills. Traditionally, the teaching of reading—especially at the intermediate level of English language learning—has focused on vocabulary development and general comprehension. The assumption has been that if a student understands the words and the structures of a reading, then that student will also understand the message of the reading. Although students may achieve some reading success following a thorough learning of grammatical forms and vocabulary items, a more efficient methodology for enhancing good reading skills exists.

Steps to Academic Reading 4, In Context actively teaches reading strategies and reading skills, integrating the many component reading skills in a rich language environment. The reading process is more than reading words and sentences: the reading process involves thinking, its connection with the student's native language, skimming for details, making judgments, understanding sequences, extracting main ideas, integrating ideas, inferencing, using context clues to figure out word meanings. These skills are learned though focus and practice.

The meaning extrapolated through the integration of these skills and the strategies learned to master them cannot be extracted through knowledge of word meaning and grammar alone. The strategies and skills must be taught and practiced, integrated into a reading process, and assimilated into a student's language repertoire gradually and naturally to become a part of the total reading process.

What are the goals of the book?

The goals and objectives of *Steps to Academic Reading 4, In Context* are to teach English language learners the reading strategies of English. Through a text arranged for contextualized, content-based learning, students can develop the following abilities:

- to tolerate a sufficient measure of ambiguity in an unknown word so that the student can recognize whether the word is the name of something, a describing word, or a verb and then to glean from the surrounding text enough information about the word to supply a general meaning. By use of such a strategy, students lessen their dependence on bilingual dictionaries and begin to feel comfortable learning words in natural language contexts.
- to skim quickly over a text to identify needed details, using context clues to locate the pieces of information

- to apply information learned from one source to the solving of a problem in another situation
- to summarize and paraphrase the aggregate of ideas that comprise a main idea
- to utilize context clues in understanding order and sequencing
- to read efficiently, increasing reading speed with full comprehension so that a student can read the 350-word timed passages included (two to a unit) in less than one minute.

How are the units organized?

There are a great number of exercises and many different types of activities in this text. However, the basic organization of the units is similar.

1. Except for the Preliminary Unit, the units begin with a pre-reading Anticipation activity that may include graphics, an invitation to survey the unit, and questions to direct the students' attention to the topic and elicit ideas, background information, and questions from them. This part of each lesson can be done profitably in class using cooperative learning principles and essential elements of instruction in brainstorming sessions, or it can be done by students individually as homework. Teachers should be aware that such brainstorming activities may be new to some students, so guiding the students in learning to predict by doing the anticipation exercises as a class activity is important at first. Most students for whom this kind of anticipation is not part of their previous educational experience will become involved actively in the process if it is clear that each students has world knowledge that can be shared with the rest of the class. Such active information gathering before the reading of the main article helps students understand that reading is a dynamic and involving activity rather than a passive endeavor. Making it fun to share ideas excites them to the learning process.

2. The second major section of each unit is the Vocabulary in Context section. In this section, the key or target words for the topic and for understanding the main article are explained in mini-contexts. The built-in redundancies may seem obvious to teacher and student at first; however, in the teaching of a skill, the first examples must be easily recognized. The goal is to separate the student from dependence on a bilingual dictionary.

3. The main reading follows next. This reading usually includes a general explication of the unit topic, but sometimes it is quite specific to one aspect of the general theme. Usually, the main reading uses the vocabulary items that have just been introduced in the Vocabulary in Context exercise. The Main Reading is the longest reading of the unit. A range of rhetorical types (analysis, case studies, description, narrative, and journalistic style) are represented in these readings.

4. A variety of activity types follow the Main Reading:

   a. **True-False** questions require reading quickly to check on answer. It is important to emphasize that knowing the answer is not enough; a student should be able to show where the answer is in the reading. For students whose native languages are written right to left or top to bottom, this practice of skimming and scanning is even more important because they need practice to train their eyes in left-to-right sweeps with accuracy, speed, and efficiency.

   b. **General Comprehension** questions of the traditional variety require students to provide information from the main reading. Because most students are already familiar with general comprehension questions, most students find their inclusion somewhat comforting: this book has some of the same things as other readers.

   c. In the **Main Ideas** section there are activities that require students to assess one paragraph or perhaps the entire reading, to consider the purpose of the writer, and to synthesize the meaning of all elements. Some activities are open to multiple interpretations. Students need to understand that the same reading might affect other students differently. The purpose of these exercises is to direct students' thinking, to involve them in negotiating meaning, and to think of what the authors' purpose might have been. Thus the main ideas section promotes critical thinking, summarizing, and paraphrasing.

   d. **Making Inferences and Drawing Conclusions** comprise another set of thinking skills. Students are asked to assess whether there is enough information to justify extensions of thought. Students learn to decide whether there is sufficient information to make an inference or draw a conclusion. Drawing the students into discussion is the best way to manage these exercises. Discussing "wrong" answers helps students clarify their thought processes as they manipulate the concepts and the language they are learning.

5. After the Main Reading and the activities that follow it, each unit has either strategy practice or related readings, both of which recycle the vocabulary and concepts. An effort has been made to diversify the contents of the units so that students stay interested. Each unit has two 350-word timed readings that respiral the concepts and give students practice in enhancing their reading speed and checking their comprehension.

6. Each unit includes a Vocabulary Journal section through which students can record and practice their lexical learning

7. Each unit includes topics for discussion, opportunities for organizing information, and writing assignment ideas. These activities, many of which can be used as homework, help students with the integrating process.

8. Specific reading strategy sections have been included, based on experience with teaching some grammatical forms.

Instructors who have used previous editions of *In Context* will find many familiar formats in this new edition, including the upbeat perspective, positive philosophy, and depth of topic. The new topics, updated articles, expanded activity formats, and integration of skills and strategies will be appreciated by students and teachers alike.

Introducing the Authors

Jean Zukowski/Faust, Ph.D., is an ESL/EFL methodologist, specializing in teaching reading and writing, a teacher, and a teacher educator. She has taught English to students in the United States, Turkey, and Poland and worked with teachers in many other places around the world. She has authored or co-authored four other texts in the Steps to Academic Reading series published by Heinle: *Steps to Academic Reading 1, Steps and Plateaus; Steps to Academic Reading 2, Out of the Ordinary; Steps to Academic Reading 3, Across the Board; Steps to Academic Reading 5, Between the Lines.* She is a professor at Northern Arizona University.

Susan S. Johnston, Ed.D., has taught and directed ESL programs in American universities in the United States and Japan for more than twenty years. Her interests include the use of technology in language instruction, content-based language instruction, qualitative program analysis, reading education, and second language curriculum development. Dr. Johnston has co-authored a number of ESL/EFL texts, including *Steps to Academic Reading 5, Between the Lines; Keys to Composition;* and the *Holt-Cassell Foundation English Series.*

Elizabeth E. Templin, M.A., is an ESL/EFL reading specialist. She has been a teacher, teacher educator, and program administrator. Her experience in teaching English to speakers of other languages extends from intensive language institutes to correctional facilities- in United States, Mexico, and Kazakhstan. She was assistant director at the Center for English as a Second Language at the University of Arizona where she now teaches.

PRELIMINARY UNIT

The Skills of Reading

In today's world, reading is the key to education. Reading is a personal interaction, like a conversation, between a reader and words on a page. As you learn to read in English, you learn new words and new grammar forms. You can learn to pronounce these English words and to understand them in their printed form. However, there is much more than that to learning to read. Reading is a process. It is also learning to use a set of skills. A *skill* is an ability to perform an act (to do something) or to make something well. For example, building something out of wood is a skill. Swimming is another skill. A person can learn to become an expert by practicing special techniques. This skill and other reading skills may be similar to how you learned to read in your first language. *In Context* will give you plenty of practice with reading skills. This practice will help you to learn English quickly and well.

In this first unit, you will get a lot of practice. You will learn to do the exercises in this book. Think how an athlete prepares to run. He or she stretches and exercises individual sets of muscles. In doing so, the athlete strengthens those muscles. Learning to be a skillful reader is much the same. You practice to strengthen single skills so that you can be a stronger reader.

Preparation

- What do you do before you even start to read?
- What do you know about the topic even before you start to read?
- How do you know about the topic before reading it?

Of course, you read the title. You look at the pictures (if there are pictures). You look to see how long the reading is. You are *preparing yourself* to read. You are *anticipating* the topic. *To anticipate* means to think about what might happen before it happens, to expect a result. The noun **anticipation** means using your own experience to guess about a topic.

Anticipation

Think about how much anticipating you do every day. For example, you look through your window to anticipate the weather. You look for signs of warm or cold, sunshine or rain. You choose your clothing according to your anticipation, your expectations, for the weather that day.

Here is another example:

This unit is called "The Skills of Reading." What information does the title give you? You learned to read in your first language. Therefore, you already know how to read! You read in your home language and also in English, but what do you know about becoming a skillful reader? Stop to think for a moment about these questions:

- What are some reading skills?
- What are some special ways that you read?
- What reading skills is this book likely to teach you?

Do you have answers to these questions? Your answers show that you can anticipate the ideas of the lesson. You know what to expect; therefore, you will find the lessons easier as you improve your reading.

In this book, each unit begins with a section called *Preparation*. In the *Topic* section, there will be a question about the subject of the reading. Then there will be some anticipation questions (*Anticipation*) and then some practice with the concepts and new words (*Vocabulary in Context*). This section will help you build your vocabulary. There are contexts (small situations) to help you learn how to use the new words and ideas. You will find several different kinds of clues or hints for the meanings of new words. You will learn how to find those clues. Learning how to use clues is called using *strategies* for learning.

Vocabulary in Context

The word *context* is probably new to you. It is an important word in this book. It's even in the title! Therefore, you need to understand it and use it. Here is an example of how a new word might be introduced—using the word *context*:

A single word can have more than one meaning (and sometimes different pronunciations). A reader chooses the correct meaning from the situation of the sentence. The word *lead*, for example, has two common meanings. As a verb, it means to help another person toward a goal, to show the way. *Lead* is also a noun. It is the name of a very heavy silver-colored metal (Pb). The *context* helps the reader choose the appropriate meaning.

A **context** is…

   a. a word.

   b. a sentence situation.

   c. a different meaning.

   d. a reader's choice.

Notice how the other sentences helped you to find the meaning. You used the *context* of the word to guess at the meaning of the word.

Your teacher will help you with the two different ways to pronounce these words.

Here are several more sentences with the word *lead* in them. Decide which meaning is right in each sentence. Is the word *lead* a verb or a noun? (Write *verb* or *noun* in the blank.) What clues help you decide?

1. There was a heavy lead pipe for the water.   *noun*

2. The lead in pencils is really a mixture of carbon and clay.   _____

3. In the circus, the clowns lead the children in a parade.   _____

4. There was a lead cap on the bottle.   _____

5. A strong person can lead others to safety in an emergency.   _____

6. The president or prime minister must lead the country.   _____

When you read in your language, you often read new words. Do you look them up in a dictionary? Probably not. First you try to guess the meaning of the word. Because the other words around the new one give you clues, you can get some idea of the meaning of the new word. This meaning is usually good enough for you to be able to continue reading with understanding. Remember too that if a writer uses a word once and it is important to the topic, that word will appear again. So read further, even if you do not know the new word. The meaning might be clearer in a few sentences. If the word is very important and you still cannot figure it out from the context, then look it up in the dictionary. It is better to learn about the word from the situation or context. You save time and you learn the word naturally.

You can learn to improve your guessing at word meanings. Here are some strategies for learning vocabulary in context. They are like clues, ideas to help you.

Vocabulary in Context Strategies

Strategy 1: Identify the word type.

Look back at the Vocabulary in Context example about *lead*. What clue did you use to find the answer? Here is more help with finding the meanings of new words by using the sentences around them.

Look at each new word carefully. Decide what kind of word it is. Is it a noun? Or a verb? Or an adjective? Or an adverb? Sometimes you can figure out the meaning—if you know the type of word.

Is it a noun?

- A noun may have an article (*a* or *an* or *the*) in front of it. [*an* orbit, *the* Earth]

- A noun may be plural and have an -*s* or an -*es* at the end. [radio*s*, printing press*es*]

- A noun could have a possessive ending. [Ben*'s* car or the Johnston*s'* dog]

- A noun may have an adjective (a describing word) in front of it and maybe a verb after it. [*the first* signal; *the* waves *travel*]

- A noun can follow a preposition. [*to* a big city; *on* a fresh horse]

Is it a verb?

- A verb follows a noun. [*Waves* travel in straight lines.]
- A verb may follow helping verbs like *can, must, may, should,* and *have to*. [A satellite *can* relay a message.]
- A verb may have an ending for third person singular (do/do*es*) or a past tense ending (walk/walk*ed*).

Is it an adverb or adjective?

- Adjectives and adverbs are modifying words, words that describe.
- Adjectives add meaning to nouns. [*three* satellites]
- An adjective can come between *a* or *an* or *the* and the noun. [the *long straight* road]
- Adverbs add meaning to verbs. [Satellites *always* seem to be in the same place above the Earth.]
- Adverbs of manner tell how an action appears, what it looks like. These adverbs often end in –*ly*. [Children dance *beautifully* and *naturally*.]

You can learn and practice several strategies, or ways to guess the meaning of words. These are clues, ideas to help you.

Practice this strategy: Is the word in **bold** a noun, a verb, an adjective, or an adverb? Circle the clue words. Note the place in the sentence too. (You do not need to know the meanings of these words!)

1. In the lab, the new **oscilloscope** is very large!   _____

2. The test included several **incredible** questions.   _____

3. She talks **unflinchingly** about the difficulties in her life.   _____

4. Nothing can **forestall** a storm.   _____

Strategy 2: Look for a form of the verb *to be.*

It is easy to find a meaning for a new word when the definition uses the verb *to be (am, is, are, was, were, has been, have been).* Here is an example:

> A *skill* is an ability to perform an act (to do something) or to make something well. For example, learning to read quickly is a skill. Sewing is another skill. A person can learn to become an expert by practicing special techniques.

> The sentences in the example actually define the word *skill. Is* acts as an equal sign (=).
> It also shows examples of the defined word; for example, sewing or learning to read.

Practice this strategy: Find the meanings of the words in **bold** print. If there is a *be* verb, underline it. Circle the meaning clues. Then write the definition in the blank.

1. To **predict** is to guess about the future. A prediction about the weather is an "educated guess." A weather reporter uses lots of information to predict the weather for tomorrow and the next day.

    To **predict** is to _____ .

2. A magazine is a collection of articles. Each **article** is a report on a topic that people will be interested in reading. Some magazines also have stories. Most magazines include advertising, too.

    An **article** is _____ .

3. The customer at the car lot wanted to check the car carefully before buying it. To **test** a car properly is to try it out first and to have an expert check it. After the driver tested the car, she decided to buy it.

    To **test** something is to _____ .

4. The **definition** of a word is an explanation of its meaning. You can find definitions in a dictionary, or you can find the meaning of a word from the context.

    A **definition** of a word is _____ .

Note that sometimes the opposite meaning is given with a *be* verb and a *not* word (like *not, neither, nor, never,* or *hardly*).

Example:

> The two houses are similar, but they are not quite the same. One is older, and the newer one is a little larger. In any case, they are nearly alike.

> Similar things are not ___*quite the same*___ but are nearly ___*alike*___ .

Example:

> Elizabeth travels out in the fields as part of her job. She needs a telephone that doesn't have wires. Her telephone isn't a regular one. She uses a cellular phone. She takes her cell phone with her everywhere.

> A **cellular phone** is one that _____ .

> What doesn't a **cell phone** have? _____

> What is a **cell phone**? Is it different from a cellular phone?

> _____

Strategy 3: Look for clause markers.

A clause might give the meaning (or clues to the meaning) of a noun. Words such as *that, which, whose, who* or *whom,* and *where* can begin a clause. You can use the information that follows one of these words to help you find the meaning.

Example:

> J.K. Rowling wrote a series of books for children. *Harry Potter and the Sorcerer's Stone*, which was the first book of the **sequence**, was instantly popular. After that she wrote several more stories that are about Harry Potter.

> In this group of sentences, a **sequence** is a series of books that were written in an order. *Harry Potter and the Sorcerer's Stone* was the first. Another is second, and so on.

Example:

> The car buyer bought the smallest car. He had looked at three cars. He thought about the price of gasoline, the size of his family, and the amount of money. His **conclusion** was that the smallest one was the best.

> In this set of sentences, a **conclusion** is a decision that a person makes after thinking about the reasons. A conclusion comes after the thinking.

Practice this strategy: Choose the best answer. Circle the letter of your answer.

1. It is useful to make **inferences**, which are conclusions from the information in a sentence. For example, a person who buys expensive running shoes is probably a runner. A person who doesn't run much would not spend a lot of money on such shoes. Therefore, guessing that the person is a runner is an inference.

   An **inference** is…
   a. like an expensive running shoe.
   b. a conclusion from other ideas.
   c. a kind of reading.
   d. an example or picture.

2. The articles in this magazine have interesting **titles** that tell readers the general subject. An article needs a good title so that readers will want to read it.

   A **title** is what…
   a. is interesting.
   b. most readers want to read.
   c. tells the subject to the readers.
   d. every article in a magazine needs.

3. *Invention* is my favorite magazine. Its **contents**, which are usually articles about science, are interesting to a scientist or a student. They are always up to date and enjoyable to read.

   Contents are…
   a. a magazine.   c. always enjoyable.
   b. topics of articles.   d. science.

4. The students learn that they probably read in several ways. For example, they do careful reading of introductions to textbooks. This kind of reading is also called "close" reading. They read stories and novels more quickly. They also need to know how to read very fast to find specific pieces of information. **Skimming** and **scanning** are the skills that most people use to read quickly to get the important information from newspapers. People use them when they are reading for details or for general ideas.

Skimming and **scanning** are the reading skills that people use...
a. to find details or general ideas.
b. to read introductions to textbooks.
c. for novels and short stories.
d. to learn to read in different ways.

Strategy 4: Look for appositives.

An appositive is a group of words with the same meaning as a noun. These words explain the noun by stating the meaning a second time. Usually there are commas before and after an appositive. (An appositive, *a group of words after a noun*, repeats the meaning of the noun.)

Example:
An **appositive**, a phrase of explanation after a word, is a kind of repetition that helps a reader to understand. An appositive is usually set off by two commas, and it can give extra, interesting information. In the following sentence, however, the appositive is an important part of the sentence. "Not many people knew that Diana Spencer, Princess Di, was nearly as tall as her husband."

An **appositive** is...
a. a repetition of the meaning of a noun.
b. extra, interesting information that follows a word.
c. a phrase or explanation after a word.
d. All of the above are correct.

In this example, all the answers (*a, b,* and *c*) are correct because all of them have at least part of the meaning of *appositive*. Therefore, the best choice is *d*. Answers *a* and *b* describe what appositives do. Therefore, they are correct. Answer *c* describes appositives. Therefore, it is also correct. This kind of answer (*All of the above are correct.*) occurs in many examinations. Learn NOW that you must read ALL the answers before you choose the *best* one.

Practice this Strategy: Choose the best answer. Circle the letter.

1. There are several steps in the **process** of reading, the series of actions that are necessary parts of reading. The steps can be explained by using an **analogy**, a situation that is similar in some ways. The reader begins to read the way a person looks at a strange food. First she looks at it carefully. She asks herself, "What does this food look like?" Next she predicts what it will be: "It looks like some kind of cake." Then she tests it; she tastes the food. The taste proves or does not prove that she was right. Reading is a similar process. A reader looks at the text. He guesses about it. He predicts and tests it. Then he finds out whether the guessing, predicting, and testing were right and goes on to the next sentence.

   A **process** is...
   a. a situation.
   b. a series of actions.
   c. a beginning.
   d. a careful examination of parts.

   An **analogy** is...
   a. a series of actions that can help a person learn how to read.
   b. a situation that can be used to explain a similar situation.
   c. a process of reading.
   d. guessing, predicting, and testing.

2. People in every country have their own **culture**, their system of beliefs and values. This system explains what they think is important and not important.

   Culture is _____ .

3. Nearly all readings have the same basic **structure**, or organization of parts. The readings begin with an introduction, a few lines about the subject. Then comes the main part of the reading. The conclusion follows at the end.

   Structure refers to...
   a. the main part of a reading.
   b. the first few lines of an introduction.
   c. nearly all readings.
   d. the organization of parts.

Strategy 5: Look for punctuation.

The fifth strategy for finding a word meaning is punctuation. Commas [,], dashes [–], quotation marks [" "], and parentheses [( )] might help you find meaning.

Example:

> Most people use the word *sentence* when they really mean a **statement**—a group of words that gives facts or information. Groups of words that ask questions are also sentences.
> A **statement** is, therefore, one of two kinds of sentences—the kind that gives facts or information. A question is also a sentence, but it is not a statement.

Practice this strategy: Complete each sentence.

1. There is a good exercise in this book on the common **marks of punctuation**—commas, dashes, periods, quotation marks, and question marks.

   Some common marks of punctuation are _____ .

2. In English, there are many useful **transition phrases**—groups of words that connect ideas. For example, the single word *therefore* and the phrase *because of this* show a cause-and-result relationship between two ideas. The words *on the contrary* mean something like *but*.

   Transition phrases are _____ .

   Some examples of **transition phrases** are _____

   _____ .

3. Understanding the general idea of a reading is a special kind of reading skill—**getting the gist**. Getting the gist is kind of like guessing. The reader gathers the key words and then makes a guess at the general idea of the reading. [pronunciation clue: /jistiŋ/]

   Getting the gist is like _____ .

4. There are many **synonyms** (words that have similar meanings) in English. A synonym for *pretty* is *beautiful*. Another word that means *big* is *large*.

Synonyms are _____ .

Strategy 6: Look around the word. Use your knowledge to guess.

The meaning of a word is usually found in the sentences around that word, not in its own sentence. The reader must try to determine which words are clues to the meaning. It is important to remember to read past the word. The writer has probably used the word more than once. Later sentences might give clues to the meaning of a word.

Remember also that the sentence itself gives you help. An *a* or *an* or *the* before the new word means that it is a noun. Also before a noun, you will find adjectives like *this, that, these,* and *another*. These words show that the idea has occurred already in the reading. You may find a clear synonym nearby. This second noun, in fact, may be a clue.

Example:

People might think that Latin is **a "dead" language** because no one speaks it today. However, anyone who studies words in English (which is not a Latin-based language like French or Spanish) knows the truth—Latin roots are still alive in thousands of words.

A "dead" language is one that…
a. is not Latin based.
b. no one speaks anymore.
c. people who study languages know.
d. is like French or Spanish.

Look in the example sentences for the answer. Why is Latin "dead" as a language? The answer is there in the first sentence: because no one speaks it today. Therefore, *b* is the best answer.

Example:

> The best *lexicons* include both the histories of words and their meanings. These books are great sources of information for a student, like other dictionaries, almanacs, and encyclopedias.

There are several reasons to guess that *lexicons* is a noun:

- the article *the* and the adjective *best* (Articles and adjectives often appear before nouns and after *be* verbs.)
- the *-s* at the end of the word (The word is probably a plural.)
- the verb *include,* after the word *lexicons* (In English, verbs usually follow nouns.)
- the word *these* must refer to something in the previous sentence, to a noun. The only possible nouns are *meanings* (which are not books), *words* (which are also not books), *histories* (which may be books), and *lexicons*. The most logical meaning is *lexicons* because it is the subject of the sentence. You can guess that lexicons are books like dictionaries. (And you are right! They are dictionary-like books.)

Practice this strategy: Find clues to determine the meanings of the words in **bold** print. Answer the questions below.

A dictionary writer has a never-ending job because language is always changing. New **terms** are needed to name new ideas. Old things develop and change, so the meanings of old words **alter**. New names are needed for new ideas. In addition, because of the **attitudes** of people, some words change their meanings completely. *Awful* is a good example. The word *awe* means "wonder and amazement; deep surprise and pleasure." Awful once meant "full of wonder and amazement." Now it means something negative. If the soup at a restaurant is awful, you don't want any to eat. Just 200 years ago, the word *nice* meant "silly." People's feelings about that word changed too. Now *nice* means "pleasing, attractive, positive." Dictionary writers have to write many new meanings, or **definitions** for words, as words change.

1. Is **term** a noun or a verb? _____ What other words are clues to its meaning? Look around the word for help.

   _____

   What does **term** mean?_____

2. Is **alter** a noun or a verb? _____ What other words are clues to its meaning? Look around the word for help.

   _____

   What does **alter** mean? _____

3. Is **attitude** a noun or a verb? _____ What other words are clues to its meaning? Look around the word for help.

   _____

   What does **attitude** mean?_____

4. Is **definition** a noun or a verb? _____ What other words are clues to its meaning? Look around the word for help.

   _____

   What does **definition** mean?_____

SUMMARY: Using Vocabulary from Context Strategies

Strategy 1: Identify the word type.

Strategy 2: Look for a form of the verb *to be*.

Strategy 3: Look for clause markers.

Strategy 4: Look for appositives.

Strategy 5: Look at punctuation.

Strategy 6: Look around the word.

Reading

The next part of every unit is a main reading. In this Preliminary Unit, the topic is reading itself. The paragraphs are numbered, so you can talk about the reading easily. After the reading, there are different kinds of exercises. You will find many examples of these exercises in the rest of the book.

The Skills of Reading

1   Let's think about reading. What is reading to you? How do you read? Well, we know that there are words on a page. We also know that we use printed words to understand ideas. And yet, there is more to reading than words on a page.

2   Reading is a process, a sequence of related actions. The first thing we do as readers is anticipate what will be in a reading. We predict what it will be about from the clues. The main clues are the titles, the pictures, and the first few sentences. How do you choose a book or an article or a topic? If you need information about the fishing industry, which of these library books do you think will be useful? Which ones will you get from the library? Which one is probably the best?

> *An Ocean Traveler*
> *How to Become a Weekend Fisherman*
> *Fish of the World*
> *The Geography of the World*
> *The Blue Planet*
> *Harvesting the Fish of the Oceans*
> *Big Boats and Small Nets*

3   Will any of these books be helpful? Which ones might have information about the fishing industry? Which ones are surely not helpful? You can tell from the titles of the books, can't you? You use your own experience to choose the best books. Reading is the same because your experience helps you become a better reader.

4   Reading is like having a conversation with a book. You interact with the text. You read a little, and you compare your ideas to what is in the book. You check your ideas with those in the book. All the testing, checking, and comparing happens very fast. It happens too fast for us to think about. If the ideas that are in the text are ideas that we expect, then everything is fine. We don't stop. However, if the ideas are not what we expect, then we stop. We pause. We think. We might change our ideas. We might read something over again. The reading process is a repetition of these steps.

5   Anticipating is just one skill. There are others that are also very important. Reading fast, or rapid reading, is one such skill. Can you read a paragraph quickly and get the information out of it? Skimming and scanning are rapid reading skills. You skim over the surface to understand the general idea of an article. You scan to look for specific information. Surveying, which is reading to understand the length and the structure, is also a kind of fast reading. Many readers survey everything they read. It helps them to know the sequence of the parts, to understand how the reading is "built." Good readers use surveying as part of anticipating.

6   Choosing the right speed is an important part of rapid reading. Perhaps you will read a newspaper fast, but some other reading tasks need more attention. Poems and reading assignments need slower reading. The introduction to a textbook must be read slowly and carefully. That's why it is important to know how, and when, to change the speed of your reading.

7   Other reading skills are related to understanding. One of these skills is understanding the main idea of a part of a reading or the whole thing. Most paragraphs have a main idea. Unfortunately, not all of them do. All the other ideas in a paragraph should be part of the main idea. Good students are able to pull out (extract) the most important ideas from a reading. They also remember them.

8   Another important reading skill is about vocabulary. A reader who can take the meaning from a context has an important reading skill. If you can get the meaning from the clues in the context, then you do not need a dictionary.

9   Understanding sequences, or the order of events, is an important reading skill. Sometimes you need to know what happened first, what happened second, what happened next, and what happened last. There are often clues to help you determine the sequence. Words such as *first, next, then,* and *finally* are such clues.

10   The last of the reading skills is using the information to make other statements about the topic. We call this skill either making inferences or drawing conclusions. The difference between them is time. We draw conclusions *after* we finish a reading. We make inferences *while* we read. For example, if a story tells us that a person needs an umbrella, we can infer that it is raining. If a story tells us that the cows are going to the barn, we can infer that the story takes place on a farm. If the story tells us that a person is wearing a warm coat because of the snow, we know that the weather is cold. Another inference is that it is winter.

11   Many people read a lot, but they do not think about the skills of reading. They simply read. If you know what the skills are, you can develop those skills. That helps you, as a new reader of a language, to think about how you read. Learning and practicing reading skills can make you a better student.

Exercises

Every main reading in this book has several kinds of exercises after it. Different kinds of exercises have different purposes. The first exercise for this reading is a **Detail Questions:** *True* or *False?* exercise. The purpose is to think about the answer and then find the sentence in the article that proves your answer. It is not enough to know the answer is true or false. You must be able to show where the answer is. In this way you will practice skimming and scanning.

Detail Questions: *True* or *False?*

Decide whether each statement is true or false according to the reading. Circle *true* or *false*. Then write the number of the paragraph in which you found the answer.

1. Surveying is reading to find out how   true   false   _____
   a reading is "built."

2. A reader makes inferences after   true   false   _____
   finishing the reading.

3. All rapid reading is skimming.   true   false   _____

4. *To extract* means "to put in."   true   false   _____

5. A sequence is an order of events.   true   false   _____

General Comprehension

This kind of question is practice with all skills. Read these questions carefully. Answer them if you can. You do not need to look at the article. If you can't remember, read just to find the answer.

1. What are two types of rapid reading?

   _____

2. What is another name for the main reading?

   _____

3. Why do most people read poems slowly and newspapers fast?

   _____

4. What words help a reader understand a sequence?

_____

5. How does surveying a reading help with anticipation?

_____

6. What happens if a reading contains ideas that surprise us?

_____

Opinions

This kind of question is "open-ended." In other words, you say what you think. There is no right or wrong answer. Students are likely to disagree.

1. Ali is a good reader in his native language, Arabic. Do you think he can learn to be a good reader in English? Why? Or why not?

2. In a college or university, a student has to do a lot of reading. Does it help to know how to read quickly, looking for specific information? Why or why not?

3. It takes about fifteen minutes to survey a unit in this book. Is that time used for a good purpose? Explain your opinion.

Main Ideas

In this kind of exercise, you will practice finding general ideas. If you know what the topic is, it will be easier to understand the new words and structures. In English, each paragraph should have a main idea. A main idea is more than one word. One word cannot tell enough about the idea to be the central idea for a paragraph. The main idea limits the meaning. In other words, how wide or how narrow is the discussion going to be?

The most common place for a main idea is in the first sentence of a paragraph. It is a good rule to follow: Write the main idea first and then write sentences that support that idea. Some writers, especially in a long piece of writing, include some introductory words first. Being able to pull out (to extract) the main idea is an important reading skill. Sometimes, for example, the main idea is not stated clearly. It is implied rather than stated. For practice, you can figure out the main ideas of each of the eleven paragraphs of "The Skills of Reading."

1. _____

2. _____

3. _____

4. _____

5. _____

6. _____

7. _____

8. _____

9. _____

10. _____

11. _____

Which of these titles could be the title of the whole reading (in place of "The Skills of Reading")? How does the title state the main idea?
a. "Reading for Meaning"
b. "Details and Sequences"
c. "Learning Skills for Reading"
d. "A Skilled Student"

Inferences

A reader can use the ideas in the reading to connect to other ideas. These related ideas are inferences or new conclusions. Words in sentences give a reader more than just their meanings.

Example:
A good reader uses the skill of surveying as preparation for reading.

Analysis: Surveying is something that good readers do.
Anticipation is an important reading skill.

Inferences: To be a good student and a good reader, the person needs to survey. Therefore, a student should survey everything before reading it. He or she can improve reading by anticipating the ideas in an article.

Read these sentences. Do you think that there is enough information in the reading "The Skills of Reading" to say whether each sentence is true or false? Circle your answers.

1. Anticipation is the skill of reading.

    a. enough information   b. not enough information

2. Surveying helps a reader understand the structure or organization of a reading.

    a. enough information   b. not enough information

3. First you read an article, and then you draw conclusions from it.

    a. enough information   b. not enough information

4. It is always best to read fast.

    a. enough information   b. not enough information

5. Making an inference and drawing a conclusion are nearly the same skill.

    a. enough information   b. not enough information

6. The order or history of an event is a sequence.

    a. enough information   b. not enough information

Vocabulary Building

There are many different kinds of vocabulary exercises in this book. Here is one type.

Fill in the blank with a word from the list. The clue words are in **bold** type.

title	survey	analogy
topic	context	strategies
extract	predict	structure
skimming	conclusions	inferences
synonyms	sequence	anticipation

1. **Thinking** about an article **before** reading it is using the skill of

    _____ .

2. **After** you have time to **think** about a whole reading, you might draw some _____ about the ideas of the writer.

3. It's not always easy to _____ the main ideas **from** the paragraphs of a reading. Sometimes they are not easy to find, so you have to **pull** the parts of the main idea together.

4. The _____ or the **name** of an article often contains clues about the main idea.

5. There are several _____ to help a new reader learn the new words in an article. If you **follow** these **suggestions**, you will find it easier to understand those words.

6. To _____ a reading, one must **look it over, beginning to end**.

7. *Large* and *huge* are _____ . They **mean nearly the same thing**.

8. I know all the parts of the movie, but I don't understand the **order** of the story. I don't understand the _____ .

9. Life is like a box of chocolates. You don't know what you'll get. This _____ is a **comparison** from a movie called *Forest Gump*.

10. It is best to learn a word from the words **around** it. Vocabulary in _____ has lots of clues to help a reader.

11. I can look at a title and the pictures and have enough information to _____ the _____ of a magazine article. I know about the **content before** I read it.

12. Every funny story is **built the same**. All jokes have the same _____ .

13. Finding one detail requires _____ a reading. By **reading quickly**, I can find a date or a name, for example.

14. First I read an article, and then I **combine the ideas with ideas of my own**. I am making _____ .

More Practice with Reading Skills

The following examples and exercises can help you with extra practice in reading skills.

Main Idea

Read these sample paragraphs. The main ideas are in different places. There is a strategy to use in finding the main idea. Look for the most general statement. The main idea is not always a sentence in the paragraph. Sometimes it is an idea from several sentences.

Example 1:

> <u>A shopper always buys more during a sale.</u> That is the opinion of a store manager at the mall. Tiffany Jackson claims that the only times shoppers really spend money are when they think they are saving money. Because Tiffany understands this idea, she plans different kinds of sales for her store every week.

> In this paragraph, the topic sentence is the first one. The rest of the paragraph is an example and explanation of the main idea.

Example 2:

> Last year every college student wore solid-colored clothes. Two years ago, black and white clothes were the most popular. This year bright colors are back, but the combinations are different. <u>It's not easy to keep up with college fashion and style.</u>

> In this paragraph, the last sentence is the main idea. All other sentences lead to that one.

Example 3:

You are on a road late at night, and your car gets a flat tire. You look for your flashlight. A child who is afraid of the dark keeps one under his pillow at night. <u>Few modern inventions are as useful as the flashlight.</u> You can find something in the back of your closet. And as a camper, you have one to light the night after the campfire has gone out.

The main idea in this paragraph is in the middle of the paragraph.

Example 4:

The notes for the paper for geography class are on top. There is a stack of books to take back to the library. I have a box of pens and pencils and all the other supplies near the wall. All my mail and some advertisements are under the books for class. Besides all that stuff, there are the notes and pieces of paper from last semester on my desk.

In this paragraph, the main idea is not stated at all. The ideas all support one main idea anyway—that my desk has many things on it.

Practice this strategy: Find the main idea in each of these paragraphs. Circle your choice of the best statement.

1. A person can always catch more fish in rainy weather. That is the opinion of Ted, an experienced fisherman. Ted says that he catches real trout only during heavy rain. Ted is a house painter, and he works only during good weather. Perhaps that explains his fishing experience.

   The main idea is that…
   a. a fisherman has to be fishing to catch fish.
   b. fish like rainy weather.
   c. Ted is a house painter who works in good weather.
   d. there is a science to catching fish.

2. In an average home library, there are a few favorite books, some unread books, and some very useful books. The dictionary is probably the most useful, but a world almanac is a close second. A good almanac includes a wealth of information about history, people, and geography. The almanac contains information about the highest mountains, the lowest valleys, the biggest cities, the deepest oceans, and the longest rivers.

The main idea is that…
a. everyone should have a home library.
b. a dictionary is not the most useful book.
c. the almanac is a useful reference book.
d. an almanac contains many different kinds of information.

3. Spiders have a bad reputation because many people are afraid of them. These eight-legged bugs build webs in houses. Because some people consider webs to be dirty and ugly, they carefully sweep away the webs and kill the spiders. However, spiders' webs catch flies, cockroaches, and other insects that bring sickness to people. Spiders actually help to keep a household healthy. Spiders are, therefore, useful, hardworking home inhabitants.

The main idea of this paragraph is that…
a. spiders are dirty and dangerous bugs.
b. spiders make dirty webs in houses.
c. spiders are helpful to people.
d. spiders enjoy working hard and building webs.

5. Have you noticed the colors around you? They may have an effect on you. For example, you may eat more food in a fast food restaurant with bright red walls. You may also eat faster. People eat less food in a room with blue walls. A room with light blue or pink paint makes people feel calm and relaxed. In contrast, some people wear black clothes to look thinner. Black sometimes makes people feel depressed. Color can make a difference in the way people feel and act.

The main idea of this paragraph is that…
a. Blue makes people eat less.
b. Color can make a difference in our feelings and behavior.
c. The colors of a building are very important.
d. People who wear black are always sad and depressed.

4. Modern tourists bring back pleasant memories of an overseas trip, but the videos often bore their friends and relatives. Cousin Sarah cannot understand why traveling is so much fun. She has never been more than a hundred miles from her home. Mrs. Brown doesn't understand the excitement of a folk dance festival. To her, the costumes are just a blur of colors. Mr. Curtis does not like the pictures of famous buildings and monuments. The videos only remind him that he does not have enough money to go anywhere.

The main idea of this paragraph is that…
a. showing a video of a trip is fun and interesting for everyone.
b. a traveler enjoys a video of his or her trip more than friends and family do.
c. folk dance festivals are colorful, and the costumes are easy to take pictures of.
d. in general, people do not like pictures of famous buildings and monuments.

Making Inferences and Drawing Conclusions

Every reader needs to understand the thinking of the writer, the author. The author tries to make all his or her ideas clear to the reader. Every word that an author uses gives the reader some information besides the "meaning" of the words. Words carry a feeling with them; these feelings give additional meaning. They *imply* more information than just the word meaning.

For example, these pairs of sentences have the same "meaning," but they have a different feeling.

a. The old man died last night.
b. The old man passed away last night.

a. She is a maid at a hotel.
b. She is a housekeeper at a hotel.

a. The baby is getting fat.
b. The baby is getting chubby.

In each of these pairs, the second sentence is a nicer way, a more positive way, of giving the same fact.

After reading "The old man died last night," what can the reader expect? Usually it will be a medical reason for his death or some other fact as information. After "The old man passed away last night," the reader expects something personal, perhaps the emotional reaction of his family.

Furthermore, there is a difference of importance between being a *maid* and a *housekeeper*. A housekeeper has a position of responsibility. (So does a maid, but being a maid isn't being important.) There is also a difference in the feelings between *fat* and *chubby*. *Fat* is a negative word; no one wants to be called *fat*. *Chubby*, on the other hand, means "cute and fat." *Chubby* has a positive meaning, especially for babies and children. There is no single rule, but the common word is usually less positive. The longer term is generally more positive.

Practice this strategy: There are four parts (A, B, C, and D) to this practice.

Part A.
Which of the sentences in these pairs implies a more positive feeling, a better attitude? Circle your answers.

1. a. He is a garbage collector.

    b. He is a sanitary engineer.

2. a. My new plant died.

    b. My new plant didn't live.

3. a. The student helped his friend on the test.

    b. The student cheated on the test.

4. a. The sick dog was killed by the veterinarian.

    b. The sick dog was put to sleep by the veterinarian.

5. a. That fashion model is thin.

    b. That fashion model is skinny.

Part B.
Read the two sentences, *a* and *b*. Draw a conclusion about which one fits. Which one should go in the blank? Write the letter in the blank.

1. a. Gwen is friendly.

    b. Gwen is not very friendly.

    _____ Everyone likes her.

2. a. Susan and Beth know each other.

    b. Susan and Beth don't know each other.

    _____ They will make a good team.

3. a. That backpack costs only twenty-five dollars.

   b. That backpack costs twenty-five dollars!

   _____ It's too expensive for me.

4. a. It is very warm.

   b. There are no leaves on the trees.

   _____ It must be winter.

5. a. This food isn't cold.

   b. This food is warm.

   _____ Let's eat it now.

Part C.

Read about some situations. What conclusions or inferences can you make from the information? Indicate all possible inferences. There may be more than one possible answer.

1. At the supermarket, Mary Lou bought three watermelons, six packages of hot dogs, six packages of hot dog buns, and five pounds of potato salad.

   a. Mary Lou must be hungry.

   b. Mary Lou is planning a picnic for a group of people.

   c. Mary Lou really likes watermelon and hot dogs.

   d. Mary Lou is on a special diet.

2. Adele spends 20% of her money on gasoline.

   a. Her car uses a lot of gas.

   b. Adele has to drive a lot.

   c. Adele's car is large.

   d. Adele buys only the most expensive gasoline.

   e. Adele works a long way from home.

   f. Adele likes to travel.

3. The professor walked into class in wet clothes.

    a. He went swimming before class.

    b. He doesn't have a clothes dryer in his apartment building.

    c. It must be raining outside.

    d. He was walking to class and the watering system for the campus went on.

    e. The weather is very hot. He was sweating a lot.

Part D.

A paragraph gives a group or set of ideas to the reader. Some conclusions or inferences can be made from the paragraph. Read these paragraphs carefully. Ask yourself if the paragraph contains enough information to make the statements. Is the idea in each statement a reasonable conclusion, an inference from the information in the paragraph? Remember, more information is implied than stated.

Circle all possible inferences. There may be more than one.

1. The honey bee, a furry flying insect, is a farmer's friend. The bee goes from flower to flower, collecting yellow pollen. The bee is collecting this raw material for honey, but it is also helping to form seeds to produce new plants next year.

   Which of these statements are implied in the information in the paragraph?

    a. Bees make pollen.

    b. Honey is made from pollen.

    c. Plants do not produce seeds if there is no pollen.

    d. Farmers enjoy honey.

    e. A farmer wants seeds.

    f. Bees like flowers for a very good reason.

2. The number of birds and bees in the world is decreasing. In the area of agriculture, many farmers use chemicals to stop the growth of weeds. The poisons that kill weeds also kill insects. That's why there are fewer bees. Birds eat insects, so there is less food for the birds. And that's also why there are fewer birds.

   Which of these statements are implied in the information in the paragraph?

   a. Bees eat birds.

   b. Chemicals that kill weeds also kill insects.

   c. Chemicals that farmers use kill birds.

   d. If there is less food, fewer animals are born.

   e. Insects die when they eat poisoned food.

3. E-mail is changing the way people communicate. Friends don't send letters anymore. They write e-mail messages to one another. One e-message can go to dozens of people at one time. So some letters are much less personal. Other e-messages are very short. The rule is this: one thought, one e-mail message. Long letters on e-mail are unusual, and the senders do not get the answers they expect. It is better to limit each message to one topic. Then the answer comes quickly.

   Which is a good conclusion?

   a. Letters as a form of communication between friends are not popular anymore.

   b. The best way to communicate is by e-mail.

   c. People communicate more but in different ways with e-mail.

   d. E-mail messages are very short.

Reading for Specific Purposes

Sometimes you read for special, or specific, purposes. Perhaps you need to find one particular fact in an article, on a list, or in a chart. Perhaps you want to know the general idea about a reading before you read the whole article carefully. By reading quickly for details and surveying for general understanding, you can find the information. IMPORTANT HINT: Always read the question carefully before you look for an answer!

Reading Quickly for Details

Strategy 1:
To find a **date**, look for numbers, capital letters, commas, and the names of months and days of the week.

Question:
When did they take the population counts? Look for the names of months and numbers.

> In 1900, the population of our town was 2,100 people. Just 50 years later, the population was over 10,000. By 1980, the town had grown to 42,000. And in this year's count, a population of 55,432 was reported.

Strategy 2:
To find a name, look for capital letters and abbreviations.

Question:
Who is the new president of the Hometown Business Owners Association?

> According to the *Daily News* Reporter, the new president of the Hometown Business Owners Association is Dorothy K. Ryder. She was chosen a week ago at the annual meeting at the Embassy Hotel.

Strategy 3:
If you are looking for a fact, notice the punctuation. Percentage marks (%), dollar signs ($), *italic* type, and "quotation" marks, for example, are useful clues.

Questions:
What was the amount of snowfall? How much money did the city lose? What happened in March?

> The Snow Mountain Ski Resort usually draws many tourists to our city. The snowfall on the mountain usually measures about three meters by January 1, but in the winter of 2000–2001, there was less than one meter by then. Furthermore, very little snow fell in January and March, and 40% fewer tourists came to town. The drop in tourist trade meant a loss of several million dollars to local businesses. Of course, it snowed ten feet on the mountain in March, but by then the tourists were going south to the beaches.

Practice this strategy: Look quickly at the chart to find the answers to the questions on the next page.

Common icons	Meaning of the symbol
a	No cigarette smoking is allowed.
b	Subway
c	Mechanic available for car repair
d	Bicycle path
e	Information here
f	Police cars at a police station
g	Traffic goes around the circle here.
h	Train station
i	Bus stop
j	Hotel or bed and breakfast
k	Restaurant
l	Parking
m	Facilities for handicapped persons

1. What are the titles of the two columns? _____

   _____

2. What three symbols show public transportation? (Write the letters of the symbols.) _____ _____ _____

3. Which two symbols are most interesting to tired and hungry travelers?

   _____ _____

4. Which two symbols are letters of the alphabet? _____ _____

5. What do these two letters mean? _____

   _____

6. One of the symbols is a "not allowed" symbol. Which one is it? _____

7. Which sign will you watch for if your car isn't working well? _____

8. Why is the bicycle path sign easy to understand? _____

Surveying

Surveying is also fast reading for a specific purpose. As you survey, you look over a whole reading. The purpose of a survey is to understand how a reading is organized.

- What are the main ideas?
- What kinds of support are there?
- What is the purpose of the article?
- How long is the reading?
- How long is the whole lesson?
- Does the article have several sections? Are they separate?

All kinds of readings can be surveyed. The purpose is to understand the structure or form first. Survey to judge an article or a lesson before you start to read it.

First read the questions. It helps you to set a purpose for your survey. Then survey the reading to answer the questions.

1. What is the title of the article or reading?
2. What information is there in each section?

Some Total Eclipses of the Sun

Sometimes the moon passes between the Earth and the sun. For a short time, the moon blocks much of the sun's light. This phenomenon is called an eclipse of the sun. There are only a few places on our planet where an eclipse can be seen. These are the areas with a "total eclipse" of the sun. The path of the eclipse is the wide strip where the moon's shadow falls.

Date of the eclipse	How long the eclipse lasted/ will last	How wide the eclipse path was/ will be in miles	Where the eclipse could be seen
April 28, 1930	0.01 minutes	1 mile	Pacific Ocean, United States, Canada
June 8, 1937	7:04 minutes	156 miles	Pacific Ocean, Peru
June 20, 1955	7:08 minutes	159 miles	Indian Ocean, Thailand, Pacific Ocean
Feb. 15, 1961	2:44 minutes	164 miles	Europe, Russia, Siberia
Mar. 7, 1970	3:28 minutes	99 miles	Pacific Ocean, Mexico, United States
June 20, 1974	5:08 minutes	216 miles	Indian Ocean, Australia
Oct. 3, 1986	0.01 minutes	1 mile	North Atlantic Ocean
July 11, 1991	6:54 minutes	161 miles	Hawaii, Mexico, South America
Dec. 4, 2002	2:04 minutes	54 miles	Southern Africa, Indian Ocean
Nov. 23, 2003	1:57 minutes	308 miles	Antarctica
April 8, 2005	0:42 minutes	17 miles	South Pacific Ocean, Colombia, Venezuela
Mar. 29, 2006	4:97 minutes	114 miles	Africa, Turkey, Georgia, Russia, Kazakhstan
Aug. 1, 2008	2:27 minutes	147 miles	China, Russia, Kazakhstan
July 22, 2009	6:39 minutes	161 miles	India, China, Pacific Ocean
July 11, 2010	5:20 minutes	161 miles	Pacific Ocean, Chile

(Adapted from the Second Edition of the *New York Public Library Desk Reference*, 1993, Stonesong Press, Inc.)

1. What are the titles of the columns?

   _____

   _____

   _____

   _____

2. How many eclipses of the sun are listed here? _____

3. How many eclipses in this list happened after you were born? _____

4. How many eclipses have not happened yet? _____

5. Which eclipse had the widest path? (Write the date.) _____

6. Which eclipse lasted the longest time? _____

7. Which eclipse in the list was the "smallest" of them? _____

   Why do you think it was the smallest? _____

   _____

8. Which eclipse could the largest number of people see? _____

Timed Readings

The timed readings in this book are approximately 350 words long. There are two timed readings in each unit. Your goal is to be able to read each of the Timed Readings in less than a minute—with 80% of your answers correct. To meet this goal, you will need to read quickly and then be able to answer 8 out of 10 questions correctly.

Here is the procedure for the Timed Readings:

1. SURVEY.
   First your teacher will give you a minute to prepare to read the article.
   *READ THE TITLE.
     What can you learn from it?
     What ideas do you expect?

   *NOTE THE NUMBER OF PARAGRAPHS.
     How is the reading organized?

   *READ THE FIRST PARAGRAPH.
     What are the key words?
     What is the main idea?

   *READ THE LAST PARAGRAPH.
     What do the first and last sentences of the last paragraph tell you?

   *LOOK FOR CLUES TO DEVELOPMENT.
     Is it a story?
     Is it a description?
     Are there many facts, names, and dates?

2. READ QUICKLY.
   Your teacher will give you a signal to get ready for the reading. When your teacher says, "Go!", read as fast as you can. Your teacher will write times (every ten seconds) on the board. When you have finished, look up at the board.

3. WRITE YOUR READING TIME AT THE END OF THE READING.
   There is a blank at the end of the reading for your time. Record your time in the blank and go quickly to the questions.

4. ANSWER THE QUESTIONS.
   Select *a, b,* or *c*—whichever best answers the question or completes the sentence.

5. CHECK YOUR ANSWERS.
   Write your time score and answer score on the record charts at the end of the book.

6. CORRECT YOUR ANSWERS.
   Work with your classmates. Do you understand your mistakes?

Timed Reading

Animal Talk

Like people, other living creatures can communicate. However, animal communication is sometimes sound communication and sometimes action communication.

A good example of action communication is the honeybee. Scientists have watched the activities of bees for a long time. One bee starts out from a beehive, the bees' home. The bee goes out to look for flowers. It finds flowers and then flies back to the hive. At the hive, the returning bee seems to move around in a dance. Other bees seem to watch. Then these bees fly out of the hive—straight to the same flowers. The first bee has somehow given information to the other bees. The bees communicated through action.

Sound communication is more common among animals. Whales in the ocean seem to "sing" to one another. Scientists have listened to whale songs with underwater microphones. They know that each whale has its own song. Scientists can recognize some whales by their songs. So far, however, scientists do not understand what the whales are saying.

Many animals—such as wild dogs, gorillas, lions, and tigers—live together in groups like families. The members of the "family" communicate with one another about proper behavior in the group. Their communication is sometimes a sound, sometimes an action, sometimes both. For example, a young wild dog will lie down in front of an older, more important dog. The young dog is communicating through the action. He is saying, "You are more important than I am."

Mother lions and tigers make gentle sounds to call their babies. They use other sounds to warn the young animals about danger. The songs of birds also carry messages. In one song they may be calling to their mates. In another song they may be saying, "This is my garden. Stay out."

Some animals seem to want to talk to human beings. For example, dolphins in the ocean often swim very close to people. They make high squeaky little sounds to the people. Are they trying to talk? Animals are talking with one another. Perhaps someday we can learn their languages, and we can talk with them too.

Time: _____

Now answer these questions as quickly as you can.

1. Animals communicate through ____ and action.

   a. bees   b. sound   c. words

2. ____ , lions, and dolphins are wild animals.

   a. Gorillas   b. Mothers   c. Scientists

3. ____ often swim close to people in the ocean.

   a. Dolphins   b. Dogs   c. Birds

4. A young dog can communicate with an older dog by…

   a. talking to the older dog.

   b. dancing in front of the older dog.

   c. lying down in front of the older dog.

5. Whales seem to communicate through…
    a. their songs.   b. a dance.   c. gentle bird sounds.

6. Human beings, whales, lions, and bees are all…
    a. scientists.   b. creatures.   c. wild.

7. An important reason for animals to communicate is…
    a. to warn about danger.
    b. to make high squeaky sounds.
    c. to be important.

8. ____ seem to communicate mostly through action.
    a. Whales   b. Dolphins   c. Bees

9. Bees live in a bee…
    a. hive.   b. garden.   c. flower.

10. The main idea of the timed reading:
    a. All creatures make sounds.
    b. Animals seem to communicate with one another.
    c. All communication is sound.

IT

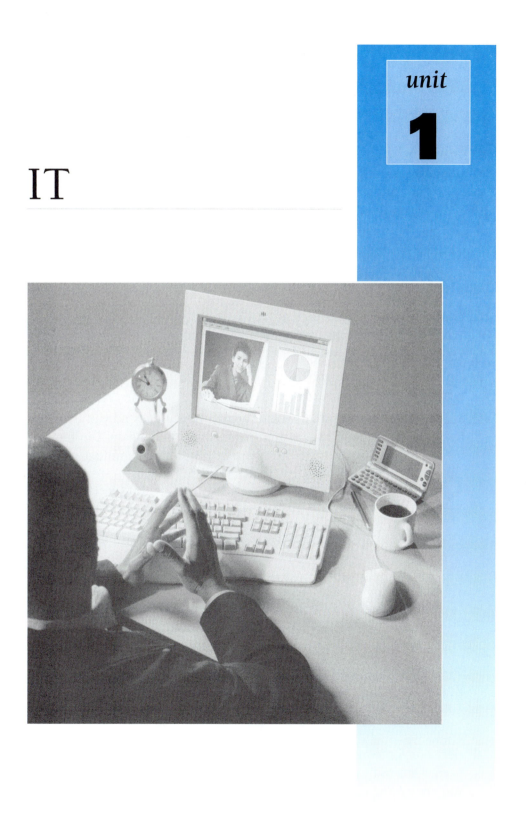

 **Preparation**

Topic

1. What is IT?

2. Survey this unit. Look at the pictures, and read the titles. What do you think the subject of this chapter will be? What ideas (clues) do the pictures give you?

Anticipation

1. The title of the first reading, or article, is "IT: Information Technology." What does this title mean to you? Explain it to a classmate, your partner for this exercise.

2. Do you use a computer? Tell your partner about your experiences with computers or the Internet.

3. Read the list of words and phrases below. Which ones do you think are important to communication and understanding? Write an **X** in the blank in front of each important word or phrase for communication. Talk about your ideas with a classmate.

   _X_ radio   _____ messages

   _____ www   _____ electricity

   _____ letters   _____ computers

   _____ surfing   _____ technology

   _____ Internet   _____ cable television

   _____ satellites   _____ cellular telephones

   _____ the news   _____ cultural differences

   _____ television   _____ speed of communication

   _____ people's different
         beliefs and values

4. Here are some more ideas about communication. Read the three paragraphs of this short reading, and answer the questions after them. You are getting ready to learn more about information technology.

About IT

1   The story of communication is an important part of world history. In prehistoric times, for example, people did not have books. They did not know much about geography. People were limited in many ways. They knew only about themselves and their environment (the land around their homes). Their knowledge of geographical things like mountains and rivers was limited. They did not travel very far. Sometimes they knew about nearby people and communicated with them. They sent messages in simple ways. Early types of signals for communication included smoke from fires and the sounds of drums.

2   Then people formed towns, and then cities, as safe places to live. Soon they began to develop other ways to communicate, to spread information. People began to buy and sell things to one another. Because of their businesses, they developed writing systems to keep records and to send messages. Life was changing for many people. Business caused changes, and so did the invention of the printing press. Many more people learned to read then.

3   Suddenly communication and knowledge improved greatly. People sent letters and news by horse and carriage. Later the mail went by train, by boat, and then by airplane. World communication became a possibility.

1. Prehistory was…
   a. many years ago, before history books were written.
   b. 200 years ago, when we had history books.
   c. after the development of the printing press.

2. People live in their…
   a. horse carriages.   b. own environments. c. businesses.

3. Mountains and rivers are geographical things. So is…

   a. smoke.   b. a drum.   c. an ocean.

4. In prehistoric times, people's knowledge of other people was limited. They…

   a. knew a lot about other people.

   b. did not know much about other people.

   c. knew a lot about geography.

5. Many more people learned to read ____ the invention of the printing press.

   a. during   b. before   c. after

6. The main idea of the reading:

   a. The story of communication is an important part of world history. (sentence 1 in paragraph 1)

   b. In prehistoric times, for example, people did not have books. (sentence 2 in paragraph 1)

   c. Then people formed towns, and then cities, as safe places to live. (sentence 1 in paragraph 2)

Vocabulary in Context

The following sentences contain some of the new words in the reading. Read each of these numbered groups of sentences. One word or group of words is in **bold**, or dark print. In the last sentence of each pair or group, find a word or group of words to show the meaning of the word or phrase in **bold**. Underline it.

1. Americans enjoy watching **soccer** games. The rest of the world calls the same game "football."

2. The radio, television, and telephone are all communication **devices**. People use this equipment to make news travel fast.

3. A radio station **transmits** messages. It receives and sends out information every minute of every day.

4. **Information** travels around the world quickly and easily. Today, sending facts and opinions in messages is no problem.

5. **Earthquakes and floods** sometimes hurt people badly. They cause a great deal of damage to houses too. Serious natural disasters like these also damage roads and crops.

6. People began to live in towns, so they wanted a **communication system**. Writing is a way to communicate. Thus, writing was the first important step in developing a way to spread information.

7. A road map looks like a spider's web of lines. Roads connect towns and cities. The lines on the map look like a fisherman's net. The map shows a **network** of roads. The connecting lines on a map show the roads.

8. They heard the news because their radio **received the signal** clearly. The signal was strong, so the radio picked it up.

9. The political leader had one firm **request**. He demanded that the television station show his speech on TV. This demand cost him a lot of money.

10. People living together need to communicate in order to share information. By **sharing information**, they can live and protect themselves better. Human development depends on people giving information and ideas to one another.

Main Reading

Information Technology

1   A soccer fan in Rio de Janeiro, Brazil, excitedly watches a soccer game. The game is being played in Australia. That's why he watches it on his television set. His favorite team wins! He jumps up and runs to the telephone to tell his wife. His wife is in a business meeting in Toronto, Canada. She cannot answer her cellular telephone at that moment, so he leaves her a voice mail message. Still excited, he writes her an e-mail message with the news: "We won!" She picks up that message instantly and writes back, "We won what?"

2   In 45 seconds or even less time, the information traveled around the world. It jumped between continents five times. The Brazilian soccer fan used three communication devices—the television, telephone, and computer—to reach his wife with the news. Each of these devices transmitted information by electrical pulses and waves. Electrical energy carried information, facts, and opinions. Of course, more significant information than sporting events can travel through these devices. Within seconds, people in many parts of the world can know the results of an election in Germany, Canada, or Japan. News of a natural disaster such as an earthquake or a flood can bring help from distant countries within hours. Even on a vacation, a businessperson can participate in a business meeting, by either teleconference or videoconference. He might first receive a report about the meeting through a fax to his hotel or directly to his portable computer. A continuously expanding worldwide network of communication systems makes it all possible.

3   Communication systems depend on electricity. When people first used electricity, it was to power light and machines. Electrical energy runs communication now. The radio, telephone, television, facsimile (fax) machine, scanner, and computer, for example, use electricity as a source of power, or energy. News and all kinds of information travel very fast on these electronic devices. The invention of the computer also changed people's lives. People can now store huge amounts of information on computers. And furthermore, the data are available to them very fast—almost instantaneously. For example, schools, hospitals, governments, and businesses keep records in computers. By pushing a few keys on a computer keyboard, people can move this information into reports and letters. Then these reports and letters—with the new data—can be immediately communicated to one, two, or thousands of people by e-mail or on the Internet.

4   Electronic messages travel in different ways. Some messages travel over regular telephone lines, and some travel through glass telephone lines using fiber optics. A fiber optics system uses long strands of glass to carry many messages at the same time. Other messages are sent by radio waves to towers. Many messages travel to satellites circling high above the Earth. The satellites transmit, or receive and send again, messages from one part of the world to another in an instant, at a speed near the speed of light. Sometimes one single message with information is transmitted instantaneously in all these ways. This causes the information to expand as it travels.

5   Information is something that grows because it is shared among groups of people. People today will never run out of information. In fact, a new problem exists for people today: They have too much information. How can they use and control all these increasing pieces, or bits, of information? A new technology, called information technology (IT), is developing to help people use large amounts of information. Some of the people working in the field of IT create and use software programs for computers to bring new information to people in useful ways. For example, office computers have programs (called "spreadsheets") that organize facts and figures quickly and accurately. Computers help to organize this new information so that people can, for instance, give more interesting speeches with graphics and pictures. Computers in hospitals arrange data to help discover causes for diseases. Governments share information about their laws, populations, and economies. Researchers in universities around the world share research. Information is being shared using IT all the time and in many new ways.

6   One of the new and common ways to share information is on the Internet. How does the Internet work? First, a person turns on his or her computer. The next step is to "log on" through a modem.

Logging on is opening a communication door. After a person logs on, a modem translates electrical information to and from the person's computer. The modem connects one computer to another computer or to an Internet service provider (ISP). An ISP is part of a telephone company or a central connection point for access to the Internet. The modem then sends the log-on request to the ISP. The ISP connects the person and he/she is "on-line." From there, two normal paths are available: A person can send and receive e-mail or explore the Internet. To follow the first path—sending an e-mail message to a friend, for example— a person writes the message, and the computer codes the message and sends it to an e-mail server. The message then waits in the e-mail server until the friend logs on to check for messages. To follow the second path—"surfing" the Internet—a person sends a site request over the Net. The request is a kind of code, like http://www.nau.edu. The information in the request helps the computer send the request to the site, or address, on the Internet. The site page then appears on the computer monitor. The Internet site also links (connects) to other sites in a similar way.

7   Using the Internet combines at least two IT communication devices: a modem and a computer. Many new communication devices combine three or more devices. Television, cellular phones, video recorders, global positioning systems (GPSes), fax machines, personal digital assistants (PDAs), scanners, and computers can work together for many different purposes. Furthermore, there seems to be no limit to the uses of communication equipment in IT. There are computer networks and networks of computer networks. These systems, and the information in them, interface (interact) with the Internet through software programs. People on Earth have more and more effective communication devices, and more and more of them interface with one another. At the same time, satellites circling the Earth create a growing net of

information traveling near the speed of light. This is all part of the large field of IT.

8 People are combining communication devices in new ways. For example, a doctor at a large city hospital can help a doctor in a small town by using a combination of communication devices. Picture this situation: A small-town doctor examines a patient physically. If the patient's illness is not easy to identify, the doctor calls or e-mails another doctor in a big city hospital. There the doctors have more resources: They can use the computerized medical library, for example. The doctor in the big city can see and talk with the small-town doctor and the patient by using a combination of telephone, television, and computer. They can see one another on TV screens and talk with the patient about his or her medical problems. Therefore, they can share a great deal of medical knowledge, or information in the medical science field, to help the sick person.

9 Another way people are using IT and many of these devices is in business. E-commerce is a quickly growing way to do business. In this approach to business, a company or person develops a Web site on the Internet to sell or buy a product or service. They advertise their product through links to other sites. They also develop and use safe ways on the Internet for people to buy things, usually using credit cards. People anywhere in the world can find the Web site and decide if they want to buy the product or service. This development is changing the way people do business.

10 The field of education is also using IT. The ITV classroom uses interactive long-distance communication. ITV means "interactive television." A Canadian teacher in a classroom in Calgary, Alberta, can communicate with some students in Singapore. Students and teacher can see one another on their television screens, talk about ideas, and share their cultures. In fact, one teacher at one university can have students in many different places. The teacher

and the students talk to one another by talking to television cameras, and their faces appear on their television screens.

11   Information technology is changing the way we do things, even the way we think. People today need to know about new developments in this field. The amount of new information available to people can be very helpful, but it must be organized and used in practical ways. People need to control the information flow to make life better on Earth.

Detail Questions: *True* or *False*?

First read each of the statements in this exercise. Then decide whether each one is true or false according to the reading. Circle *true* or *false*. Also write the number of the paragraph with the answer in the reading.

1. The Brazilian soccer fan used six communication devices to reach his wife with the news.

   true (false)   _2_

2. Communication systems use electricity.

   true   false   _____

3. A flood is a natural disaster, and so is an earthquake.

   true   false   _____

4. Fiber optics uses long pieces of fabric, or material, to communicate messages. Information grows.

   true   false   _____

5. An ISP is an integrated system printer.

   true   false   _____

6. Communication devices do not usually work together.

   true   false   _____

7. Medical information is difficult to store on computers.

   true   false   _____

8. It is not safe to use credit cards on the Internet.

   true   false   _____

9. Information can be used without   true   false   _____
   organization.

10. IT refers to Internet Teaching.   true   false   _____

General Comprehension

Read each question carefully. Perhaps you can answer it without looking at the reading. It is all right to do so. Perhaps you need to look in the reading about information technology to find the answer. If so, then read quickly— just to find the answer. Key words are in **bold**. The number in parentheses is a paragraph number (where to look for the answer).

1. What are some examples of **communications devices**? (1, 2, 3, 7)

   _____

2. What does fast **communication** mean to people in a **disaster** area? (2)

   _____

3. How did the **invention** of the **computer** change people's lives? (3)

   _____

4. What are some of the things **IT** (**information technology**) can do? (4, 7, 8, 9, 10)

   _____

5. How does **e-mail** work? (6)

   _____

   _____

6. How can a **university class** with one teacher be offered in many countries at the same time? (10)

   _____

   _____

Opinions

Here are some ideas from the reading and some ideas about the topic. Read each one, and then ask yourself these questions:

- Do I agree with the sentence or group of sentences?
- Do I disagree—do I think that it is wrong?
- Am I not sure?

Read the sentences. Write a check (✓) under *I agree, I disagree,* or *I'm not sure.* Then work with a classmate. Do you and your classmate have the same answers? Why or why not?

1. Rapid communication brings help fast after a disaster, and this is good.

   ❑ I agree.   ❑ I disagree.   ❑ I'm not sure.

2. Sending a message by e-mail is better than sending it by mail.

   ❑ I agree.   ❑ I disagree.   ❑ I'm not sure.

3. A computer is like a bank. People store money in a bank. And they store information in a computer.

   ❑ I agree.   ❑ I disagree.   ❑ I'm not sure.

4. Computers can store too much information about people's lives.

   ❑ I agree.   ❑ I disagree.   ❑ I'm not sure.

5. Life is becoming more impersonal because of IT.

   ❑ I agree.   ❑ I disagree.   ❑ I'm not sure.

6. Slow, careful communication is usually better than fast communication.

   ❑ I agree.   ❑ I disagree.   ❑ I'm not sure.

7. Rapid communication causes change. Many people are afraid of change.

   ❑ I agree.   ❑   I disagree.   ❑   I'm not sure.

8. People can avoid problems by using technology.

   ❑ I agree.   ❑ I disagree.   ❑ I'm not sure.

9. People who use the Internet know more than people who do not.

   ❑ I agree.   ❑ I disagree.   ❑ I'm not sure.

10. Life was easier without technology.

    ❑ I agree.   ❑ I disagree.   ❑ I'm not sure.

Main Ideas

One of the statements best states the main idea or gives the key words of each paragraph. Circle the letter of that item.

1. The main idea of paragraph 1:

   a. The example shows the importance of the television set as a communication device.

   b. The example shows how to communicate with electronic devices in Brazil, Australia, and Canada.

   c. The example shows how people use many different communication devices in everyday life.

2. The main idea of paragraph 2:

   a. The growing networks of communication systems around the world carry all kinds of information, facts, and opinions.

   b. The Brazilian soccer fan used three communication devices—the television, telephone, and computers—to communicate in 45 seconds or less.

   c. News about disasters can bring help from distant countries within hours.

3. The main idea of paragraph 3:

   a. Data can be immediately communicated to thousands of people by e-mail or on the Internet.

   b. Large amounts of information can be stored on computers.

   c. The invention of electricity and computers changed people's lives.

4. The main idea of paragraph 4:

   a. Communication satellites circle above the Earth.

   b. Fiber optics uses glass telephone lines.

   c. Electronic messages travel in different ways.

5. The main idea of paragraph 5:

   a. Information technology (IT) helps people share information in useful ways.

   b. People today will never run out of information.

   c. Spreadsheets organize facts and figures quickly and accurately.

6. Paragraph 6 mainly explains how a person…

   a. makes the Internet work.

   b. sends an e-mail message.

   c. surfs the Internet.

7. The main idea of paragraph 7:

   a. Software programs interact with the Internet.

   b. Communication devices can be used together for many different purposes and in many different ways.

   c. Information travels at a speed near the speed of light.

8. The main idea of paragraph 8:

   a. By combining telephone, computers, and television, doctors at different places can work together to help a sick patient.

   b. Libraries can be computerized to help doctors save patients' lives.

   c. Doctors work hard to save patients' lives.

9. The main idea of paragraph 9:

   a. A Web site is necessary to do e-business.

   b. People can buy things safely with credit cards using the Internet.

   c. Information technology is changing the way people do business.

10. The main idea of paragraph 10:

   a. The faces of the teacher and the students appear on the television screen.

   b. Because of information technology, teachers and students can be in very different places and communicate directly using television cameras.

   c. Students can share thoughts about their different cultures.

11. The key phrase in paragraph 11:

   a. life better on Earth

   b. new developments

   c. information technology

Vocabulary Building

Recognizing Words and Abbreviations

Match each word or abbreviation in the list with a phrase below. Write the letter of the word or abbreviation in the blank in front of the phrase. If you find the word or abbreviation in the reading, it will help you. Use the paragraph number next to each one.

a. GPS (7)
b. Internet (6)
c. ISP (6)
d. IT (5)
e. http://www.nau.edu

f. ITV (10)
g. log on (6)
h. modem (6)
i. software (5)
j. www (6)

1. __*j*__ World Wide Web

2. _____ programs that run computers

3. _____ interactive television

4. _____ information technology

5. _____ Internet service provider

6. _____ open a communication door

7. _____ global positioning system

8. _____ Web site address

9. _____ connects one computer to another or to an Internet service provider

10. _____ many networks connected around the world

Understanding Word Use

Because communication and information technology are changing so quickly, people need new words to talk about computer things and activities. Sometimes they use old words in new ways. Match the sentences with the **bold** words with the way the word is also used now. Write the letter in the blank space. You may use some of the answers more than once.

a. the pattern of many interconnections of electric signals and sites on the Internet.

b. an address on the Internet for some Web pages.

c. exploring the Internet; visiting one site and going to another site.

d. an electronic passage or way to go from point to point on the Internet.

e. an electronic connection between two or more Web sites.

f. a series of connecting lines between two electronic places.

1. ___c___ **Surfing** used to mean riding waves in the ocean on a board. Now it also means…

2. _____ A **net** used to mean strands of string tied together. Now it also means…

3. _____ A **web** used to mean the very thin strands a spider makes to catch insects for food. Now it also means…

4. _____ A **site** used to mean an actual place, a piece of ground. Now it means…

5. _____ A **link** used to mean a metal ring that connects to other metal rings to make a chain. Now it means…

6. _____ A **path** used to mean a trail or a way through a woods or field that people walk on. Now it also means…

Finding Words in Context

Practice with words and learn more about them. Look at paragraph 6. This paragraph explains how a person might use the Internet. This paragraph shows a process. It shows how to do something.

Use paragraph 6 to help you fill in the blanks in the following chart. Also, use the words below for help. Some of the words can be used more than once.

links	logs on	writes	e-mail server (n.)
waits	site (n.)	explores	sends and receives
sends	turns on	connects	
codes	appears	request (n.)	

1. A person...

   a. _____ to his or her computer.

   b. _____ through a modem.

2. The modem...

   a. _____ electrical information to and from the computer.

   b. _____ the log-on request to the ISP.

3. The ISP...

   a. _____ the person, and the person is "on the Net."

   4. Two possible paths...

   A.
   1st path:

   B.
   2nd path:

   a. _____ e-mail

   a. _____ the Internet

   b. A person...

   _____ the message

   b. A person...

   sends a _____ request

   c. The computer...

   _____ the message

   c. The computer...

   sends the _____ to

   the site

   d. Then the computer...

   sends the message to an

   _____

   d. The site page...

   _____ on the computer

   monitor.

   e. The message...

   _____ for the

   friend to check for messages.

   e. The Internet site...

   _____ to other sites

   in the same way.

 ## Vocabulary Journal

As you go through each unit of *In Context*, you will learn many new words. You can make them your words by keeping a vocabulary journal.

Find a notebook with 50 to 100 pages. You will use this notebook for your own vocabulary journal. Give it a title, write your name in it, and carry it with you to class every day.

Your personal vocabulary journal will be a record of the words that you want to learn. Each day, ask yourself the following questions:

- What are the new words in this unit?
- How many do I already know?
- Which words are useful new words for me?

Then follow these directions every day:

- Choose five of the new words for your vocabulary journal. (These are your target words.)
- Find your target words in the Main Reading.
- Copy the five sentences in which your target words appear.
- For each new word, you will need several lines, perhaps half a page in a small notebook.
- On the first line, write the target word.
- On the second line, copy the sentence (or, if you like, the sentences) in which your target word appears.
- On the next line, write a definition.
  Is the target word a noun?
  Is it a verb?
  Is it an adjective or an adverb?
  It might even be a word that is more than one type of word!
  What does it mean?
  What are the singular and plural forms?
- Then write a sentence or two of your own with the target word. If you are not sure of the new word, ask your teacher. It's also a good idea to look up the target word in a dictionary.

You are on your way to improving your vocabulary! You can learn twenty-five new words every week, and use them every day!

Example: A useful new word in Unit 1 is *device*.

For *device*, the vocabulary journal will look something like this:

<u>device</u>

The Brazilian soccer fan used three communication

<u>devices</u>—the television, telephone, and computer—

to reach his wife with the news.

<u>Device</u> is a noun. The plural form is <u>devices</u>. A

<u>device</u> is a machine that does a simple job.

<u>Examples:</u>

The fax machine is a <u>device</u> for sending copies of

papers over the telephone lines.

I have lots of different <u>devices</u> in my kitchen.

This <u>device</u> sharpens pencils fast.

I need a better <u>device</u> than my alarm clock to

wake me up in the morning.

Structure Focus

Before or *After?*

Each numbered item contains two sentences. The two sentences are about events. One event happened first. Combine the two sentences, using *before* or *after*, to make one good sentence. You may change the words in the sentence— if you need to. Write your sentences on your own paper.

> Example:
>> People lived on farms.
>> They lived in towns.
>
> Combined: *Before people lived in towns, they lived on farms.*

> Example:
>> The printing press made books for everyone.
>> Many more people learned to read.
>
> Combined: *After the printing press made books for everyone, many more people learned to read.*

1. The printing press was invented. There were few books for people to read.

2. The fax machine was invented. People could send letters in an instant.

3. I pushed a few keys on the keyboard. The printer made a copy of the e-mail message.

4. Communication became very rapid. The world seemed smaller.

5. Communication became faster. Business became better for international companies.

6. People began to travel. They knew only about their parts of the world.

Related Reading

A Shrinking World

1   Communication today is almost instantaneous—it happens with great speed. It is interesting to note how the speed of communication changed the world. To many people, the world has become smaller. Of course, the world is really still the same size physically, but it seems smaller.

Two hundred years ago, communication among the continents and over the oceans took a long time. News went with the ships and took weeks or even months to cross the ocean. It took six weeks at least for news from Europe to reach the Americas, and it took even longer for information from Asia to reach Europe.

2   This time difference influenced people's actions. For example, one battle, a fight between soldiers in the War of 1812, happened after the signing of a peace treaty. The leaders had signed a peace agreement in England, but the news of peace took six weeks to reach North America. During that time many people lost their lives in the Battle of New Orleans, an American city. There would have been no battle with faster communication. In the past, communication took much more time than now. The world seemed much larger then.

3   Today people have new responsibilities because of the speed of communication. World leaders often have to make fast decisions; they must send messages without much time for considering other possible answers to their problems. As a result, the leaders may have only minutes, or at most a few hours, to consider all parts of a problem. The world expects immediate answers. In the past, world leaders had days and weeks to think before making decisions.

4   Because of the speed of communication, people can learn more about one another. People can learn to listen to one another, to try to understand one another's beliefs and values. Because of communication, it is possible to learn about other people's ways of living. It is not necessary to accept others' values, just to understand them. Two cultures may be different, but one is not better than the other. They are simply different.

5   Cultural differences may cause serious problems. For example, the question of time is different between one group and another. People of one culture may value time, so they are always on time for appointments. They do not understand lateness. People of some other cultures may not pay attention to clocks. Lateness is not a problem for them. Because of technology, these people can learn about one another and avoid misunderstandings. Communicating between or across cultures is important. In a sense, the world has become smaller because of technology. Therefore, people can learn to communicate better, not just faster.

Detail Questions: *True* or *False*?

Read each statement and circle *true* or *false*. Also write the number of the paragraph with the answer.

1. Before the 1800s, news from England took   true   false   _____
   six weeks to reach the Americas.

2. The world seems larger today than   true   false   _____
   200 years ago.

3. New Orleans is a city in Europe.   true   false   _____

4. A battle of the War of 1812 happened after   true   false   _____
   a peace treaty had been signed.

5. Technology helps communication.   true   false   _____

6. The War of 1812 was between England   true   false   _____
   and France.

7. News travels faster today.   true   false   _____

8. The size of the world has changed   true   false   _____
   physically.

9. Today communication across the ocean   true   false   _____
   is instantaneous.

10. Today leaders have more time to make   true   false   _____
    decisions.

Opinions

Read the sentences. Write a check (✓) under *I agree, I disagree,* or *I'm not sure.*

1. Misunderstandings happen because people do not communicate well
   enough.
   ❑ I agree.   ❑ I disagree.   ❑ I'm not sure.

2. It is important to be on time.
   ❑ I agree.   ❑ I disagree.   ❑ I'm not sure.

3. It is good to understand other people.
   ❑ I agree.   ❑ I disagree.   ❑ I'm not sure.

4. There are better ways to solve problems than battles and wars.
   ❑ I agree.   ❑ I disagree.   ❑ I'm not sure.

5. Faster communication is better communication.
   ❑ I agree.   ❑ I disagree.   ❑ I'm not sure.

6. A letter is sometimes a very good way to communicate.
   ❑ I agree.   ❑ I disagree.   ❑ I'm not sure.

7. It was better to have a larger world.
   ❑ I agree.   ❑ I disagree.   ❑ I'm not sure.

8. All countries should have peace treaties with other countries.
   ❑ I agree.   ❑ I disagree.   ❑ I'm not sure.

Vocabulary Building

Choose the best word or words to complete each sentence. The words in **bold** type will help you.

1. **Differences** between one culture and another can cause misunderstandings. One group of people has different ____ from those of another group.

   a. houses   b. books   c. values and beliefs

2. I want to **avoid** that examination. I ____ it!

   a. don't want to take

   b. don't want to spread

   c. don't see

3. Asia, Europe, Africa, North America, South America, and Australia are six of the seven **continents**. Antarctica is the only ____ without people.

   a. city   b. land mass   c. ocean

4. A **shrinking** world is ____ .

   a. getting smaller   b. getting hotter   c. growing larger

5. Today world leaders do not have much time to **consider** their decisions. They have no time ____ them.

   a. to fight about   b. to think about   c. to help

6. The leaders were happy and proud of the new peace **treaty**. Their ____ brought a stop to the fighting.

   a. agreement   b. technology   c. problems

Discussion Ideas

Talk about communication with a classmate. Share your ideas with the whole class.

1. Why does the world seem smaller today?
2. How has faster communication changed people's responsibilities?

📖 Related Reading

Principles of Fiber Optics

1   It is not always easy to understand inventions and new developments in science. To understand fiber optics, however, you can try an experiment. You need a glass of water, one or two drops of milk, a piece of black paper, a piece of white paper, a flashlight, and a dark room. The light of the flashlight must be bright. Make a black paper collar for your flashlight. Use the piece of black paper. In the middle of it make a hole with the tip of a pencil. Put the black paper cover over the head of the flashlight. (See Figure 1.1a)

2   Put a drop or two of milk into the glass of water. Turn off the lights. Shine the light from your flashlight through the top of the glass at an angle of about 45 degrees. (See Figure 1.1a) Put the piece of white paper against the glass where the beam of light is shining. Move the paper so you can see where the beam is coming out of the glass. You should see a spot of light. Some of the light has passed through the water and through the glass. You see it on the paper. You also see another beam going down into the glass. It is being reflected down into the glass.

Figure 1.1a

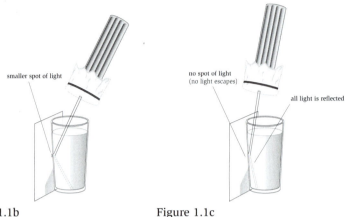

Figure 1.1b   Figure 1.1c

3   Next move the flashlight so that the beam is coming straighter down (30 degrees) into the water. (See Figure 1.1b.) You will see the same phenomenon: some of the light is reflected back into the glass. And some escapes out. Now move the beam of light from the flashlight slowly up until you cannot see any light escaping. (See Figure 1.1c.) This point is called the "point of total internal reflection." The word *internal* means "inside." All the light is staying inside the glass. There is no beam showing a bright spot on the white paper. All the light energy is inside the glass.

4   The glass of milky water is like a strand, or string, of glass. A fiber optic tube is a bundle of long thin strands of glass, really many tubes. However, the principle is the same: at a certain angle, all the light energy that goes into the glass fiber comes out the other end.

5   Light is energy. Sound is energy. Radio waves and electricity are both energy. They can all be changed into light, and as light they can all travel along a glass fiber. Light travels at the rate of 186,000 miles per second. Therefore, a message can travel that fast in a glass fiber. This is the principle, or law of nature, that makes fiber optics work.

Vocabulary Building

Complete the sentences with words from this list.

tube	strand	energy	reflection
fibers	angles	degrees	experiment
beam	bundle	principle	

1. Look at Figure 1.1 These pictures show an _____ .
   Someone is trying to prove something.

2. Look into a box. It has several corners. Each corner is made up of
   _____ . They are usually 90 _____ .

3. Look into a mirror, and you will see your _____ .

4. Electricity is really just _____ , but we can
   make it do lots of work.

5. The clouds covered the sky, but then an opening appeared and a
   _____ of sunlight shone through it.

6. Fiber optics is a system for carrying information. It uses a
   _____ of glass fibers, not wires.

7. After the rain, the water ran off the street through a large
   _____ .

8. The cloth, or material, in a dress or shirt is made of natural
   _____ —usually cotton, linen, wool, or silk.

9. One string of a material is called a _____ .

10. One of the most important laws of nature is the _____
    of gravity: things fall to Earth.

Writing Ideas

Make a list of communication devices that you use every day. Now go back in time two hundred years. Compare life today to life then. What changes are a result of better communication? How is your life different? How has communication changed people's lives?

Organization of Ideas

With your classmates, make a list of ways to send messages—both modern and prehistoric. Then arrange them in order, from the oldest to the newest.

Discussion Ideas

Talk with your classmates. Discuss these questions:

1. Why do we need technology?
2. How can communication make life better?
3. Do you know of any new technologies that you think will make life worse?
4. Can information travel too fast? Can too much information cause problems?

Timed Reading 1

Remember to survey first, to mark down your reading time, and to record your score on the questions.

The Mail Must Go Through

Letters have always been an important way for people to communicate. In the early days of American history, there was a great distance between population centers. There were big cities with lots of people in the East, and many people lived in the far West. However, there were only a few cities in between. In any case, there were some people in Boston, Massachusetts, who wanted to communicate with family and friends in San Francisco, California. Their letters were carried on ships, but the ships sailed around South America, a trip of several months. Of course, people wanted a faster way to communicate. Faster communication has always been a goal.

On April 3, 1860, the Pony Express began. The Pony Express company had 400 fast horses and 80 young men to ride the horses. The riders of the Pony Express carried mail between Saint Joseph, Missouri, and Sacramento, California. The railroad tracks ended in Missouri. The mail went by train as far as Saint Joseph. From there it was carried by these brave horseback riders. A typical rider was a young man. He carried the mail in a leather saddlebag. He rode the horse very fast for 12 miles, or 18 kilometers. Then he changed horses and rode a fresh horse to the next station. There were 190 stations for the Pony Express. They were 12 to 15 miles apart. Each rider rode about 75 miles or 121 kilometers.

A fresh rider waited for the tired rider at the end of his ride. Then this new rider took the mail and a rested horse to the next station.

The Pony Express riders rode day and night. They rode in the rain and the snow. Their motto was "The mail must go through." The distance between Saint Joseph and Sacramento is 1,966 miles (3,164 kilometers). Mail took ten days by Pony Express. The horsemen went much faster than ships. However, after eighteen months, the Pony Express ended. The telegraph system between the East and West Coasts started. Technology then carried information faster than the men and horses of the Pony Express.

Time: _____

Now answer these questions as quickly as you can.

1. There were ____ stations on the Pony Express.
   a. 12   b. 1,966   c. 190

2. More than ____ riders carried the mail from Saint Joseph to Sacramento.
   a. four hundred   b. eighteen   c. seventy-five

3. The riders rode about ____ miles a day.
   a. 200   b. 75   c. 15

4. The Pony Express had 400 ____ .
   a. stations   b. horses   c. riders

5. The Pony Express ended after ____ years.
   a. 75   b. 12   c. one and a half

6. The mail reached ____ in ten days by Pony Express.
   a. Missouri   b. Sacramento   c. Saint Joseph

7. The typical Pony Express rider was ____ .

    a. from Boston   b. a young man   c. from Missouri

8. At a station, a rider always ____ .

    a. picked up more letters.

    b. stopped to rest.

    c. got a fresh horse.

9. The motto of the Pony Express was ____ .

    a. "The mail must go through."

    b. "Saint Joseph to Sacramento in ten days."

    c. "Pony Express riders go day and night."

10. The main idea of the reading:

    a. The Pony Express ended in 1861.

    b. The Pony Express carried mail between Saint Joseph and Sacramento.

    c. Information travels faster by telegraph than by horse or ship.

Timed Reading 2

Communication by Satellite

High above Earth there are communications satellites. Rockets take them high into the sky, usually about 22,300 miles or 35,900 kilometers above Earth's surface. Like the moon, Earth's only natural satellite, communications satellites travel in a great circle (an orbit) around our planet. Most of these satellites travel at the same speed as the Earth, so they seem to be always in the same place in the sky. Stations on the ground, called Earth stations, send signals to these satellites. They carry equipment to relay (send on) the signals. Because of these satellites, communication can be both easy and rapid.

The first communications satellites were like sound or signal mirrors. Like a person looking in a mirror, the returning signal was a reflection of the first signal. Messages bounced off the satellite like a ball on a road.

Today, however, communications satellites are active devices. They receive the signals, amplify or strengthen them, and relay them. The communications satellites over the Atlantic Ocean can carry more than 100,000 telephone calls at one time.

As these satellites circle the Earth, messages are sent to them with radio waves (microwaves). Waves like radio signals travel in straight lines. Using a satellite to receive and then transmit the signal (that is, relay the message), technicians are sure that the messages will continue. The waves travel in a straight line up to a satellite and then in a straight line down to Earth at an angle. Because there are a large number of these communications satellites, a message can go up and down as many times as necessary to reach anyone anyplace on the planet. One satellite at 22,300 miles above the Earth can send signals to about one-third of the planet. Therefore, with three satellites in the proper places, messages can go every place on Earth. Satellite communication happens so fast that it is almost instantaneous.

These satellites make it possible for an event in one part of the world to be seen on television everywhere. Telephone calls between any two places on Earth are now possible.

Time: _____

Now answer these questions as quickly as you can.

1. Communications satellites travel into the sky by ____ .

   a. satellite   b. rocket   c. moon

2. An orbit is a great ____ .

   a. moon

   b. speed

   c. circle around the Earth

3. Signals go to the satellites from ____ .

   a. Earth stations   b. telephones   c. the moon

4. The first satellites were like ____ for signals.

   a. mirrors   b. reflections   c. messages

5. A ball ____ or reflects off a road.

   a. amplifies   b. bounces   c. relays

6. Communications satellites can carry ____ telephone calls at the same time over the Atlantic Ocean.

   a. about ten   b. 22,000 miles   c. more than 100,000

7. Microwaves are ____ waves.

   a. radio   b. ocean   c. slow

8. One satellite can send signals to ____ of the planet.

   a. about half   b. all   c. a third

9. The distance of 22,300 miles is the same as ____ .

   a. 35,900 kilometers

   b. the moon's orbit

   c. the distance across the Atlantic Ocean

10. The main idea of this reading:

    a. Radio waves travel fast and can carry messages.

    b. Instant communication is possible because of communications satellites.

    c. The moon is the only natural satellite of Earth, but there are now many more satellites in orbit above the planet.

WATER
PLANET

📖 Preparation

Survey this unit. Look at the pictures. Guess what the topic is about.

Topic

1. What do you know about planets?
2. Do you know that water is rare among the planets?
3. Do you know which one has a lot of water on it?
4. Why is the water probably very important?

Anticipation

1. Consider the title. Why is it the Water Planet? Circle all the reasons for the name.

    a. Water in the oceans covers 70 percent of Earth's surface.

    b. The great polar ice caps (at the North and South Poles) are frozen water.

    c. The clouds above the planet are water in the form of gas.

    d. The air has water in it as a gas.

    e. The land masses of Earth (the continents) have water in lakes, in rivers, in streams, and deep in the rock.

    f. Without water, the Earth would not have life on it. Because there are many kinds of life on the planet, the name "Water Planet" is appropriate.

    Did you choose all the reasons? If you did, you were right! Water makes life on Earth possible, and water is everywhere. Look at the drawing of the water cycle on page 77. It shows that water is always changing form. Most of Earth's water is in large bodies of water like the oceans, lakes, and rivers. Some is in water-bearing rock, deep under the surface of land. This water is called groundwater because it is under the ground. In the form of ice, there is water high on mountain tops. In the extreme northern regions of North America, Asia, and Europe, there is a lot of snow. At the "top" and "bottom" of the planet at the North and South Poles, there are ice caps. The third form of water is water in the air. This water is called water vapor (gas). Most of the water as gas is invisible. Some of it, however, we can see as clouds. The water falls out of the clouds as rain or snow.

2. On the drawing of the water cycle, write the names of as many parts as you can. Look in the paragraph on page 76. Find the necessary words. For example, notice that *ocean* and *groundwater* are already on the picture. Then make a list of vocabulary about water here:

_____

_____

3. Discuss: Why is water so important to us? What do you use it for?

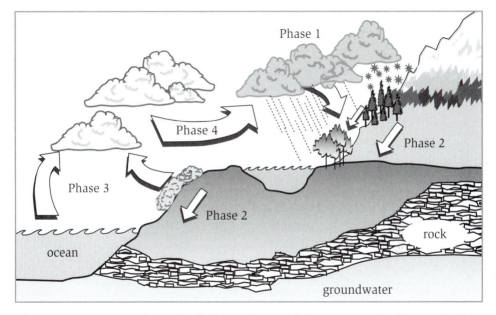

The same water goes through all these phases of the water cycle. Nature, in fact, recycles water—uses water over and over again. The amount of water on the Earth does not change. All these states, or forms, of water are natural. One day a molecule of water is a gas in a cloud. On another day, it is a liquid, and it falls as rain. Then it is part of a drop of water in a river. A few days later it is in the ocean. That same molecule may become a gas again when the sun hits the ocean surface. Then the molecule of water rides in the air, up to a cloud. And the cycle starts all over again.

Phase 1: FIRST, water falls as rain.

Phase 2: THEN, water runs off the land toward an ocean, OR water seeps through the soil to become groundwater—that is, water under the ground.

Phase 3: NEXT, water evaporates from the surface of the ocean and goes into the air.

Phase 4: SOME of that water vapor forms rain clouds. The clouds cool, and they drop water as rain.

4. Think about the words *nature* and *natural*. **Nature** refers to the world and all parts of the world, without any human changes. **Natural** describes all things that people have not made. Are the things in the list below natural? Write *yes* in the blanks in front of all the natural things. Write *no* in front of things that people have made.

_____ ice	_____ ocean	_____ clouds
_____ the world	_____ seas	_____ words
_____ houses	_____ computers	_____ lakes
_____ streets	_____ the soil	_____ mountains
_____ cows	_____ the air	_____ the sun
_____ cities	_____ the Internet	_____ horses
_____ the land	_____ cell phones	_____ rivers
_____ people	_____ groundwater	_____ buildings

5. Nature uses water over and over again. **Using something over and over is recycling.** Nature recycles water. What do people recycle? Do you recycle glass? Aluminum? Plastic? Paper?

6. We want the water of the Water Planet to stay clean. Therefore, we should "Reduce, reuse, and recycle." *Reduce* means we should use less. *Reuse* means we should use it again, make it work longer. *Recycle* means we should use old materials to make new materials (use the materials over and over again). In each of these three contexts, the person is reducing, reusing, or recycling. Write one of these three words in each of the blanks.

   a. Art and Virginia Brown have a large vegetable garden. They want to save these vegetables to eat during the winter. Every fall they wash out their glass jars and use them to can (preserve) vegetables from their garden. The Browns are _____ the jars.

   b. Charlotte Acker is a careful shopper. She knows that the customer pays for the packaging on a product. She avoids products in expensive plastic containers. She also buys large sizes of the products. In this way, she is _____ the waste of plastic wrapping and containers.

c. Bill and Angela Williams are careful with all waste materials. They save paper; they stack their old newspapers. They also collect all the glass bottles and jars from their groceries. They do not throw them away. They save steel and aluminum cans too. One day each month, they take the cans, paper, and glass to the _____ center. They believe in _____ everything. (Use the same word two times.)

Vocabulary in Context

The following sentences contain some of the new words in the readings of this unit. The sentences will help you to learn how to figure out the meanings of words that you do not know. Find clues to the meanings of the words in **bold** type and <u>underline</u> them.

1. Nine <u>heavenly bodies</u> circle the sun. The closest to the sun is Mercury. Next comes Venus. The Water **Planet**, Earth, is next, and then comes Mars. After Mars, there is a belt of tiny planets called asteroids. The really large planets come next: Jupiter, Saturn, Uranus, and Neptune. Far, far away, is the last of our sun's natural satellites, a tiny planet called Pluto.

   What clue or clues did you underline?

2. The blanket of air around Earth protects the surface from the rays of the sun. Planets without the covering of air are dry and hot. Nothing can live on those planets. Without a thick **atmosphere**, every living thing on Earth would die from the heat and dangerous rays.

   What clue or clues did you underline?

3. A river **flooded** every year. The spring rains and melting snow caused it to flow over the banks of the river and onto the streets and fields. The people of the region wanted to control the water. Therefore, engineers built a large dam to hold back the water and to store it for dry times. This **reservoir** was also used as a lake, for swimming and boating. The danger of floods is reduced too. The high water of the river cannot destroy crops.

   a. What clue or clues did you underline for *flooded*?
   b. What clue or clues did you underline for *reservoir*?
   c. What clue or clues did you underline for *flood*?

4. The dinner table was set: there were plates, water glasses, and food on it. But the family dog **upset** the table. She ran under the table and caused it to turn over. Everything fell on the floor. Water spilled everywhere. The man used a towel to **absorb** the water on the floor. Soon the floor was dry, and he set the table again.

   a. What clue or clues did you underline for *upset*?
   b. What clue or clues did you underline for *absorb*?

5. A car accident happened because of a storm. The driver was driving down the road. Suddenly, the storm began. Within minutes, it was raining hard. The driver could not see the road clearly. He had to slow down. The rain **interfered** with his driving. Then a dog ran across the road. The driver had to turn quickly to avoid the animal. He lost control of the car, and he hit a fence.

   What clue or clues did you underline?

6. There is a **balance** of everything in nature. There is never too much water in the ocean or too much water in the air. The right amount exists (is) in both places.

   What clue or clues did you underline?

7. The city water department made a plan for recycling water. **Sewage** water, the dirty water from homes and factories, can be cleaned and **filtered** to keep parks green. There are large pipes, called **sewers**, that take the water to a treatment plant. The water passes through screens, or **filters**. The filters remove all the impurities. The water is clean enough to water grass.

   a. What clue or clues did you underline for *sewers* and *sewage*?
   b. What clue or clues did you underline for *filter* and *filtered*?

8. Where do people get the water for everyday uses? Some people live near a natural water source, like a lake, a river, or a **spring**. Lake and river water is on the surface of the Earth. That's why it is called surface water. Spring water, however, is groundwater. This water comes to the surface from under the ground by itself. In some places there are no springs or surface water. People have to dig for it. A deep hole for water is a **well**. **Underground** water is usually clean. It has **seeped** through, or slowly passed through, sand and rock, which have filtered it.

   a. What clue or clues did you underline for *spring*?
   b. What clue or clues did you underline for *well*?
   c. What clue or clues did you underline for *underground*?
   d. What clue or clues did you underline for *seeped*?

Main Reading

The Water Planet

1   The astronaut looked back at home and exclaimed, "Earth looks like a big blue marble." From high above the Earth and from the surface of the moon, the planet gleams and shines. The blue water in the oceans and seas of the Earth makes an interesting picture. The white clouds above the Earth add beauty to the picture. Water is not only a source of beauty but also the source of life on Earth. It is the reason that people can live on this planet. Water is everywhere. It is in the atmosphere, the air that people breathe. It is in the soil, the ground that grows the food. Water is in deep underground rock, in natural reservoirs, in storage. In a real sense, water keeps Earth alive.

2   Nature has an unchanging amount of water. Furthermore, nature has a perfect system for recycling water. Water is used again and again. It falls as rain. Then it goes to one of three places. It might seep slowly through the soil; it soaks through the ground into the natural reservoirs in the rock. It might disappear into the air by evaporating quickly—by becoming vapor, or gas. It might run off into streams, rivers, and oceans. By itself, nature can keep the balance and provide plenty of clean water for us. Nature recycles water.

3   There is one serious problem, however. People cause problems for this natural recycling system. The water cycle is a balance that can be easily upset by people. Nature's recycling system can work well only if people work with the system, and not against it. Some ways that people interfere with nature are easy to understand. For example, dirty sewage water from homes and factories must not mix with drinking water. People get sick from drinking polluted water. Sometimes water from factories goes into

streams and rivers. It seeps into the underground water. It can flow into lakes, too. This kind of industrial pollution (wastewater from factories) can be dangerous for people. Water that runs off the surface of farmland can also contain dangerous chemicals. Any water that contains poisons and chemicals is poison. These poisons make people sick; some poisons kill people and other living creatures. Without knowing, people can upset nature's recycling system through pollution.

4   Lakes and rivers add beauty to the world, and people enjoy water for recreation purposes, too. People enjoy swimming and playing in the cool water of a lake in the hot summer. They like to ride on boats on the rivers. Many people enjoy catching fish from the rivers. They fish for food and for sport. However, in some places, the water of the lakes and rivers is no longer safe. These rivers and lakes are polluted. The fish are dying because of the chemical poisons from farms and factories. In addition, people cannot swim in polluted water. Two examples in North America are the great Mississippi and Potomac rivers. A lake that is now becoming polluted and dangerous is Lake Michigan. The balance of nature is upset; people have interfered with nature.

5   There are other ways that people interfere with nature. Some of these ways are not easy to understand. For example, of what use is wetland? No one can plant crops on it. No one can build a house on it. Therefore, engineers have drained the wetlands in order to make useful land. Many shopping centers stand on dry land today, land that was once wet and marshy. Yet the soft and wet ground of bogs serves an important purpose in nature. In a marsh, surface water can soak slowly down through the soil into the underground rock. The underground reservoir, nature's storage tank, fills slowly with that clean, filtered water.

6   Why is less water seeping into underground reservoirs? Housing developments and shopping centers cover much of the

surface of the Earth with asphalt and concrete. Water cannot seep through these hard surfaces. Rainwater cannot soak into the ground because of the buildings, roads, and parking lots. So it floods parking lots and flows into the basements of homes. To solve this problem, engineers build huge storm sewers to carry the storm water away. However, these sewers cause another problem. They carry all the water away. Not much water can seep into the underground reservoirs. The once unlimited supply of fresh, clean water is now limited. Nature's recycling system is in danger. What is happening to the Water Planet?

7   Because of water, Earth is a living planet. People can live here because of water. They build large dams to store water in huge reservoirs. The water in these artificial lakes can irrigate farmland and provide water for cities. Furthermore, water from the reservoir flows down through large pipes in the dam. This moving water is very powerful. Water from the dams can make electricity. Electricity from water power is called hydroelectricity. Examples of hydroelectric projects are the Grand Coulee Dam on the Columbia River in Washington State in the United States, the Aswan Dam in Egypt, and the huge James Bay hydroelectric project in Quebec, Canada.

8   These hydroelectric projects produce electricity for the people of nearby cities and towns. However, these dams also cause problems. In some places, the reservoirs behind the dams have destroyed the environment for animals, birds, and plants. In other places, the dams have changed the nature of the river. For example, on the Columbia River between Washington and Oregon, a dam has caused the water in the river to rise, to get deeper. The level of the river rose, and now it covers Celilo Falls. Native Americans once fished at the falls. Now the water is very deep, and the people cannot fish there. The dam not only changed the river, but also changed people's way of life, their culture.

9   In Egypt, the huge Aswan Dam produces electricity and controls the floodwaters of the Nile River. These purposes are two positive reasons for a dam. However, there are negative sides to the dam too. The yearly flooding of the Nile River valley once made the land along the river very rich. The river water carried new soil to the valley. Now there are no more floods, and the land is not as rich.

10   The situation is similar in Quebec. There are both positive and negative aspects to the James Bay project. It drains water from three large rivers and adds it into a fourth, the La Grande. All the water makes one very powerful super-river. When the La Grande flows through the hydroelectric plant, it produces a lot of electricity for the people of Canada. However, changing the flow of rivers upset the environment and affected people's way of life. Many of the native people are not happy about the project because of the changes to the environment and to their culture. Scientists cannot predict all the results of a project like James Bay. Many of Quebec's animals and plants may die because of the project. Poison from plants that are already dead under the water may affect the fish. Another result may be flooding in the largest river system of the whole North American continent, the Missouri-Ohio-Mississippi River system. The Canadian and United States governments and the officials of the native people have been studying the effects of this project on the environment. Probably the project will not be finished as it had been planned. They know that a change in one system affects other systems. Everything must be in balance.

11   One fact does not change: the balance of nature on the Water Planet is easily upset. And upsetting the natural water cycle makes lots of problems for people. All people share these problems. Water gives life to the planet, so people must learn to live in balance with nature, or the shining planet Earth will die.

Detail Questions: *True* or *False*?

Decide whether each statement is true or false according to the reading. Circle *true* or *false*. Also write the number of the paragraph with the answer in the reading.

1. There is water everywhere—even in the soil.   true   false   _____

2. Oceans are huge underground water storage places.   true   false   _____

3. There is nothing that people can do to upset the balance of nature.   true   false   _____

4. Nature has a purpose for marshy bogs—to let water seep into the underground water places.   true   false   _____

5. Storm sewers help nature recycle water.   true   false   _____

6. Houses that are built on marshy land are likely to have wet basements.   true   false   _____

7. Nature's supply of pure water is unlimited.   true   false   _____

8. Flowing water can make electricity.   true   false   _____

9. Celilo Falls was once part of the Columbia River.   true   false   _____

10. All the native people in Canada like the James Bay project.   true   false   _____

General Comprehension

Read each question carefully. If you can answer the question without looking at the reading, do so. If you need to look in the reading for the answer, check the number in parentheses beside the question. It is a paragraph number. Read as quickly as you can to find the clues to the answer.

1. What makes life possible on our planet? (1) _____

2. Rainwater disappears into three places. What are these places? (2)

_____ _____ _____

3. There is water in the air. What is it called? How does it get there? (2)

   _____

4. Name two rivers that are polluted. (4)

   _____ _____

5. Name one positive and one negative result of a storm sewer. (6)

   _____ _____

6. What can stop water from seeping into the ground? (6)

   _____

7. Some great rivers have dams on them. The water of these dams makes hydroelectricity. Name one of the dams. (7) _____

8. What are four ways that people have upset the balance of nature? (all paragraphs)

   _____ _____

   _____ _____

Opinions

Read each sentence and check (✓) *I agree, I disagree,* or *I'm not sure.*

1. People could live on a planet without water.
   ❏ I agree.   ❏ I disagree.   ❏ I'm not sure.

2. People must cooperate with, or work with, nature to help the water cycle.
   ❏ I agree.   ❏ I disagree.   ❏ I'm not sure.

3. Sewage water is dangerous to people.
   ❏ I agree.   ❏ I disagree.   ❏ I'm not sure.

4. Building on marshy land is a good idea.
   ❏ I agree.   ❏ I disagree.   ❏ I'm not sure.

5. People must limit their use of asphalt and concrete.

   ❑ I agree.　　　❑ I disagree.　　　❑ I'm not sure.

6. Dams are dangerous.

   ❑ I agree.　　　❑ I disagree.　　　❑ I'm not sure.

7. Hydroelectricity is a positive purpose for building a dam.

   ❑ I agree.　　　❑ I disagree.　　　❑ I'm not sure.

8. Polluted rivers can never be clean again.

   ❑ I agree.　　　❑ I disagree.　　　❑ I'm not sure.

Main Ideas

Read each of the following questions and circle the letter of the correct answer.

1. Choose the main idea of this reading.

   a. Nature is all living things.

   b. People must not build housing developments and shopping centers.

   c. Water is important to people everywhere.

   d. All people must work to keep the environment clean.

2. Which of these ideas is the conclusion of the reading?

   a. People must work together to keep the Water Planet alive.

   b. There are no problems with keeping water clean.

   c. The water cycle is a natural part of the Earth.

   d. Rain washes the Earth, and so it is clean.

Inferences

Which of these statements are probably true, based on the information in this main reading? Write an *X* in the blank in front of all the possible inferences.

   _____　Rivers with dams are dangerous.

   _____　A reservoir can be a source of water and also an area for recreation.

   _____　Water does not seep through hard surfaces like asphalt and concrete.

_____ Marshy bogs are an important part of the water cycle.

_____ The sand and soil under the surface of the Earth act like filters for water that seeps down into the underground reservoirs.

Vocabulary Building

In each line of the exercise, there is a group of three words or phrases. One expression in each group is different. Find the word or phrase that does not belong to the group. Circle it. Make sure you can explain your answer.

Example: air   (breathe)   atmosphere

(*Air* and *atmosphere* are the same: Earth's atmosphere holds the air, and the air is the atmosphere. *Breathe* is a verb; it means taking in air.)

1.	run off	evaporate	disappear into the air
2.	soak	seep	breathe
3.	reuse	balance	use again
4.	storage	reservoir	groundwater
5.	well	spring	stream
6.	dam	lake	ocean
7.	engineer	cooperate	work together
8.	soil	ground	water
9.	reason	answer	purpose
10.	wetland	marshy bog	storm sewer

Vocabulary Journal

Choose five words from the Vocabulary in Context list to be your target words. Write the words here:

_____ _____ _____ _____ _____

Now write them in your vocabulary journal. Remember to include the following parts:
- your target word
- the sentence from the Main Reading in which your target word appears

- a definition, including the part of speech
- some sentences of your own

Discussion Ideas

Discuss the following questions. What are your opinions?

1. People affect many parts of nature. What are some of the ways that people change nature? Are these changes good or bad?
2. What is pollution? What kinds of pollution are there? Which kinds of pollution can you stop?
3. What can people do to help nature return to a balance?

Structure Focus

not only..., but also...

A. In the Main Reading, there are two sentences that use *not only..., but also....* This pair of phrases always goes together. The words before *not only* are not repeated after *but also*.

- Water is *not only* a source of beauty, *but also* the source of life on Earth.
- The dam *not only* changed the river, *but also* changed people's way of life.

The meaning is like *and* or *too*, but there is also a sense of emphasis. Use *not only..., but also...* to join these pairs of sentences together:

1. The sun is the source of our light. It is the source of all energy.

   _____

2. Our planet is the Water Planet. It is the only living planet.

   _____

3. The North and South Poles have very cold temperatures. They have lots of snow and ice.

   _____

4. There is water in the oceans. There is water in the form of ice and water vapor.

   _____

5. There is water in underground rock. There is water as ice on mountain tops and on the poles.

_____

B. In these example sentences, the verbs are different. When the verbs of the sentences are different, the subject and verb in the first sentence switch places, often using *do* or *does* as a helping verb.

   Example:

   The astronaut stepped out onto the surface of the moon. He looked back at Earth in surprise and wonder. = Not only did the astronaut step out onto the surface of the moon, but he also looked back at Earth in surprise and wonder.

   Use *not only..., but also...* to join these pairs of sentences together:

1. Water forms clouds. It falls as rain or snow.

_____

2. Farmland can cause water pollution. The waste from factories pollutes many bodies of water.

_____

3. People should be careful about where they build houses. They must protect marshy bogs.

_____

Related Reading

States of Matter

1   Nature is the Earth, and everything on Earth is a part of nature. There are many things to see on Earth—the sun, the sky, the ground, and the water. All of these things are parts, or **components**, of our world. They are natural parts of where we live, our **environment**.

2   There are living and nonliving parts of our environment. Living things on Earth are divided into two groups. These groups are the two "kingdoms." Each living thing is a component of either the animal kingdom or the plant kingdom. Animals are living beings that can move and breathe oxygen. Plants are living things that take in carbon dioxide (CO_2).

3   Some nonliving things, such as rocks, are minerals. Because of these nonliving **substances**, or **materials**, animals and plants can **exist** on our planet. The plants need the minerals to make food. The plants make food from the mineral components of Earth. The animals eat the plants, and the waste products go back into the soil. This example shows the **food cycle**. All natural parts of our world depend on the other parts to continue existence. If one part is taken away, the balance of nature is in danger. Everything on Earth is part of a balance. Nature is a **balanced** system. For example, if there are too many animals in the forest for the amount of food, some of the animals die. Then the amount of food increases, and more animals are born.

4   One important part of the balance of nature on Earth is water. Life on this planet would not be possible without water. Water is a life-giving **substance**. Usually we think of water as a liquid. As a liquid, it fills the lakes, rivers, and oceans of the world. Water is important in another form: as a **solid**, as ice. Huge amounts of water are stored as ice in the cold areas of the Earth, at the far north—in Canada, Alaska, Greenland, northern Europe, and Siberia—and at the far south, in Antarctica. These two "ends" of the Earth, the areas of the North and South Poles, are called ice caps. Water is in the air, too, as a gas that we cannot see. **Liquids**, **solids**, and **gases** are the three natural states of matter. Each thing in existence on this planet takes one of these three forms. Only water has all three forms naturally on the planet.

Vocabulary Building

Can you figure out the meanings of the words in **bold** in this reading? Write the word that means the same as the word in **bold**. Choose the words from the list below. Some words may be used more than once.

gas	liquid	material	component
solid	cycle	existence	environment
state	matter	substance	
exist	balance	food cycle	

1. What are the three natural forms of matter?

   _____*liquid*_____ _____*solid*_____ _____*gas*_____

2. a. Ice is one form of water. Another word for **form** is

   _____ .

   b. Which two words mean the same as **matter**?

   _____ _____

3. a. One of the words means the same as **live** or **be**. Which word is it?

   _____

   b. What is the noun form of this word? _____

4. Which word means nearly the same as **part**? _____

5. Which word means nearly the same as **circle**? _____

6. All parts of the Earth are made up of _____ .

7. In nature, there must be a _____ among all living creatures and the amount of food available for them. Animals eat plants, and waste products go back to the soil. This is the

   _____ . Nature is a _____ cycle.

8. The word for our **surroundings**, the land around us, is

   _____ .

General Comprehension

Think about the ideas in this unit. Also, think about examples from your experiences.

1. What are some parts of the animal kingdom that you know?

    _____

2. Name some parts of the plant kingdom.

    _____

3. What are some of the minerals on Earth?

    _____

Related Reading

A River Runs Through It

1   Before a person does something, he or she cannot know all the results. Scientists, for example, worked hard to put satellites into orbit around the world. However, they did not, could not, imagine some of the results of their work. Not only do we have space stations in orbit, but we also have the Hubble Space Telescope. We even have cameras to photograph our planet.

2   An unexpected result of satellite photographs came from Landsat, a satellite that does remote sensing. *Remote* means "far away," so **remote sensing** is seeing or feeling things from a distance. Landsat also takes **high-resolution** photos. These photographs show a great deal of detail.

3   A scientist named Dr. Farouk El-Baz was studying a Landsat photograph of the Arabian Peninsula. He noticed an interesting line on the photograph. It runs from the Hijaz Mountains to the Nafud Desert. Then the line disappears. This line is actually a deep valley. At a point 110 miles across the desert, El-Baz saw

another line. This line is actually a dry channel. The channel goes across the desert to the sea at Kuwait.

4   El-Baz drew a line on the photograph to connect these two lines. On one side of his line, he saw long and narrow hills of sand. On the north side of the line, these dunes all have the same shape. On the other side, the south side of the line, the hills are not long and narrow, but dome-shaped. What could explain the differences in the dunes? How could El-Baz explain his line through the desert? He tried to explain it with an interesting theory. El-Baz believes that the reason for the differences in the sand dunes was a huge river. A river 5 miles (about 8 kilometers) wide and 50 feet (almost 16 meters) deep would cause both the line and the dunes. The deep valley in the mountains and the valley through Kuwait, he thinks, were both part of a river bed. El-Baz made an educated guess. He used the evidence to make a theory. The existence of a river is his hypothesis.

This is a copy of the actual satellite image that Dr. El-Baz studied. Find the line that Dr. El-Baz noticed. It is the line that starts at the top of the picture. This line shows a deep valley. At the bottom of the picture, you can see the sand dunes—on the left they are long and narrow, and on the right they are short and dome-shaped.

5   But when did this river run? According to El-Baz, between 6,000 and 11,000 years ago, the last ice age ended on Earth. At that time the Arabian Peninsula was quite wet, and there might have been a river. El-Baz calls it the Kuwait River. Approximately 5,000 years ago, this river dried up.

6   El-Baz will continue this research. With space equipment, he will try to locate the river banks. The scientists have also been looking for evidence of earlier civilizations. They have used the information from the satellite to locate the ancient city of Ubar. There is another great hope: perhaps there is still a river there, underground. Water in the Nafud Desert would help the people of that dry area very much. If El-Baz finds water, then water will be another benefit of space research.

Main Ideas

This reading has both a main idea and a theme (general idea). What idea that is more general than the title is in the reading?

  a. Most rivers in the world run underground.
  b. The results of one kind of research may affect another.
  c. Satellites help communication around the world.
  d. Sand dunes show the location of underground rivers.

Vocabulary Building

Look in the reading for definitions for the words in **bold**. Write them in the blanks to finish the sentences.

  1. Landsat has **remote** sensing equipment. These devices can find water

     on Earth from a _____ .

2. There are **hills of sand** on one side of the line. These hills are dome-shaped. On the other side, however, the _____ are long and narrow.

3. Landsat is a kind of **space station**. High-resolution photographs from this _____ can show scientists details about the Earth.

4. The deep _____ across western Arabia joins a **channel** across eastern Arabia and Kuwait.

5. Farouk El-Baz's **educated guess** is that a river once flowed across the desert. Now he will do more research to test his _____ .

Detail Questions

Look in the reading for numbers, words beginning with capital letters, and words in **bold** to fill in the blanks.

     According to _____ El-Baz, there was once a river on the _____ Peninsula. El-Baz was studying a photograph from _____ , a satellite that has _____-sensing equipment. This satellite also takes _____-resolution photographs. El-Baz called this river the _____ River. It ran from the _____ Mountains to present-day Kuwait. It was about _____ kilometers wide and _____ meters deep. It formed during the last ice age, between _____ and _____ years ago. Unfortunately, it dried up about _____ years ago.

Discussion Ideas

1. a. You use water for many things. List five of them.

   _____ _____ _____

   _____ _____

   b. Next read these questions. Then discuss your answers with a classmate.
      • How much water do you need for each use?
      • What would you do with only half this amount of water?
      • How can you change what you do now to save water?

2. Think about the green grass on a golf course. What makes it green? Golf courses can pollute groundwater. How? How are golf courses like farms?

Writing Ideas

A year is like a cycle. It starts at one point and ends at the same point. Write a paragraph. In your paragraph, explain the school year cycle or the cycle of the seasons.

Organization of Ideas

Let's brainstorm! As a class, think about the balance of nature. On the board, make lists of two different kinds of activities. Some activities are positive; they help nature's balance. Other activities are negative; they upset nature's balance. What changes can you all suggest?

Timed Reading 1

Water Changes Things

In 1997 and 1998 unusual weather conditions existed around the world. For example, in the United States, Chicago and New York had very warm winters with almost no snow. At the same time, in the deserts of the American Southwest (places like New Mexico, Colorado, Utah, and Arizona), it rained more than usual. There were hurricanes in the Pacific Ocean, but not in the Atlantic, although there usually were. Down south in Australia, there was a drought. The lack of rain caused great hardship for the people. For instance, several wildfires damaged the land.

Asia experienced difficult weather conditions too. The Yangtze River in China was so low that boats could not travel up the river in August and September. In South America, heavy rains caused landslides in Ecuador, Bolivia, and Nicaragua. Many people lost their homes, and others lost their lives. The years 1997 and 1998 were bad for many parts of the world.

Moreover, scientists are predicting other serious changes. Hurricanes in the Atlantic Ocean will be more disastrous. In the Pacific Northwest, the conditions will be good for the salmon in the Columbia River because of more rain. The rivers of China will be full, while South America may have drought conditions.

Years of research mean that now scientists know more about weather cycles. The water in the oceans becomes warmer or cooler in cycles of years. We are now in a warming cycle. It began about 100 years ago, and it will probably continue for several centuries. Marine biologists and other scientists have been studying the coral reefs in the southern oceans. These scientists know that sea animals build the coral reefs near the shores of continents. Scientists study how coral grows. It grows more when water is warmer and less when water is cool. The scientists see a pattern in the growth of the coral. The pattern shows the temperature changes of the water. The coral reef is like reading a book about the history of the weather. Changes in the temperature of the water in the oceans cause changes in the weather and events around the world.

Time: _____

Now answer these questions as quickly as you can.

1. Changes in the weather and events around the world are often caused by...
   a. sea animals.
   b. landslides.
   c. water.

2. Coral reefs grow...
   a. along the Yangtze River.
   b. in cool water.
   c. in the southern oceans.

3. In 1997, there were more hurricanes...
   a. in the Pacific Ocean.
   b. in the Atlantic Ocean.
   c. near Africa.

4. Riverboats could not travel up a river in…

   a. South America.

   b. Bolivia.

   c. China.

5. After 1998, conditions will be good for…

   a. salmon.

   b. coral.

   c. scientists.

6. Scientists see a pattern in the…

   a. rivers in China.

   b. growth of coral reefs.

   c. deserts of the Southwest.

7. In 1997 and 1998, there was no drought in…

   a. Australia.

   b. Nicaragua.

   c. the American Southwest.

8. Heavy rains cause…

   a. coral reefs.

   b. landslides.

   c. wildfires.

9. When the water is warm,…

   a. coral grows faster.

   b. coral grows less.

   c. coral stays the same.

10. The warming cycle began…

    a. two centuries ago.

    b. in 1997.

    c. about 100 years ago.

Timed Reading 2

Stopping the Spread of Deserts

Look at a globe or a map of the world. Find the deserts. Notice where they are. Most of the deserts lie between 15 degrees and 30 degrees north or south of the equator. This region is called the desert belt. These dry areas, like the Sahara, the Kalahari, the Gobi, and the Nubian, are getting larger, and they are growing fast. The spread of dry useless land is a serious problem. Because the number of people in the world is increasing, the need for food is also becoming greater. Crops cannot grow in a desert, so people must stop the growth of deserts. The world needs more usable land for farms, not less.

Scientists are trying to find a way to stop the spread of arid land. Then they can find ways to fight back. They are trying to understand the reasons for desert spread.

Thus far, scientists have identified three reasons. The most important reason for the spread of deserts is the climate pattern of the world. Weather systems, especially the winds, over the desert areas dry out the land. Second, there are few rivers, so there is nothing to replace the lost water. In addition, people have changed the land. Simple changes can upset the balance of nature in a desert—a desert is a fragile environment. However, people have needs. For example, people need food; they must clear land for fields to plant crops for food. However, they leave the land without the natural protection of plants, and winds can dry the land.

A third reason for the spread of deserts is the number of animals. People want animals for milk and meat, but there are too many animals for the fragile environment of these areas. Hungry animals eat the grass, even the roots. They leave the land bare. Then the land is not protected against the dry winds.

People cannot change the climate, but they can protect the land. They can plant trees and grasses and limit the number of animals, too. People can be careful in their use of water and stop the spread of deserts.

Time: _____

Now answer these questions as quickly as you can.

1. A globe is a…
   a. desert belt.
   b. serious problem.
   c. kind of map.

2. Which phrase describes a desert?
   a. an arid area
   b. clear land
   c. trees and grass

3. One reason for the spread of deserts is…
   a. too much rain.
   b. dry winds.
   c. floods.

4. You can find most dry areas of the world…
    a. near the equator.
    b. near the ocean.
    c. in the United States.

5. Deserts spread because of…
    a. animals, trees, and rivers.
    b. weather, storms, and floods.
    c. climate, people, and animals.

6. People must clear land…
    a. for rivers.
    b. for their animals.
    c. to make fields.

7. Bare land…
    a. is good for animals.
    b. is unprotected.
    c. has trees on it.

8. A fragile environment…
    a. is always bare.
    b. is dry.
    c. can be easily upset.

9. What does *arid* mean?
    a. a hot, dry wind
    b. growing
    c. dry

10. The main idea of this reading:
    a. Animals are hungry.
    b. Deserts are growing, and it is a serious problem.
    c. Simple changes can upset the balance of nature.

DIFFERENT VIEWS ON EDUCATION

 Preparation

Topic

Look over this unit. What are the parts of the unit? How is it organized? What do the titles and pictures in the unit tell you about the unit? Find the Main Reading. What is the title? How many paragraphs are there in it?

Anticipation

1. Think about all the schools you have gone to. Were they all the same? How were they different? Why were they different?

2. What kinds of things do you find in a school for little children? What is a high school or a university classroom like? Why are there so many differences?

3. How do children learn? Do they watch adults and then copy them? Do they learn by listening to a teacher? Do children learn by doing things for themselves? What difference does it make for teachers?

4. Which of the following ideas are likely to be part of this unit? Write *likely* or *unlikely* in the blank in front of each statement. It is important to be able to explain your answers.

   a. _____ Education is important for many people.

   b. _____ There are many ways to get a good education.

   c. _____ There is a kind of education that is holistic—it teaches the whole child.

   d. _____ A good education is the key to a successful future.

   e. _____ There are many places to visit in the world.

   f. _____ A college campus is a center of learning.

   g. _____ Doctors must go to school for many years.

   h. _____ An education can cost a lot of money.

■ Vocabulary in Context

The following sentences contain some of the new words in the reading. Read each of these numbered groups of sentences (contexts). One word or group of words is in **bold**. Find clues in the context to the meanings of the words in bold and <u>underline</u> them.

1. Children naturally watch their parents. They see how their mothers and fathers act, and they copy them. Good parents show by example the best way to act. Good parents are good **models** for their children.

2. Common shapes are circles, squares, triangles, and rectangles. These **forms**, however, are not often found in nature. Nature uses softer lines.

3. Learning to add numbers and to write sentences are parts of every child's education. Other **aspects** are learning to read and learning to think clearly.

4. Children love to hear stories about fairies and animals that talk. They also enjoy **tales** about famous people.

5. In kindergarten, children learn to be with other children. They learn to work with others, to wait for permission to talk, and to follow the rules of the school. Without kindergarten, a child might not understand the **discipline** of going to school.

6. Wax from beehives becomes soft in a person's hand. The warmth makes the wax soft enough to make different shapes out of it. Children enjoy **molding** it into animals and other shapes.

7. Some children are good at dancing. Some do very well in reading. Other children **excel** in mathematics.

8. What is the connection between learning and wanting to learn? Most teachers agree that there is a strong **link** between the two because children who want to learn, learn best.

9. A teacher with many years in a classroom came to watch and help a new teacher. She **observed** the class for two days. Then she and the new teacher met to talk about the class.

10. Together the experienced teacher and the new teacher discussed the problems in the classroom. They **analyzed** the children's behavior and came up with ideas on better ways to work with the students.

11. Some ideas are positive. They are suggestions that make people feel happy and hopeful. Other ideas do not give a person a good feeling. The person feels bad or maybe sad. These are **negative** ideas.

12. Some children become afraid easily. They do not welcome changes. They **shy away from** things that they do not understand.

13. One child in the class does not understand how to add. He doesn't seem to be able to learn how, either. The teacher wants to fix this problem. So she is giving him **remedial** work to do. Perhaps it will help him learn.

14. Not understanding a lesson can give a child stress and worry. A special lesson for a child who doesn't understand might help the child. However, being separate from the other children can also be a learning **trauma**. It might make a child dislike school.

Main Reading

Holism in Education

1   The question of the best way for children to learn is as old as civilization. For most people, this question refers to *what* children must learn. Some people believe that children should be taught the important facts of history and know details of great literature. Other people believe that children should learn math, chemistry, physics, biology, and computer science first. At this time in world history, schools and schooling is big business. And, unfortunately, few people are paying attention to how children learn best.

2   Should someone show children how to do a task? Should someone tell a child how to do it? The Greek teacher Socrates believed in asking young people questions. In this way, they can find their own answers. Aesop believed in telling stories with lessons in them. The lessons become part of a child's mind. Great teachers like Confucius believed in teaching the rules.

All these great teachers had part of the secret to good teaching. Rudolf Steiner, an Austrian philosopher and teacher (1861–1925), put many of the ideas together with a special view of the child. In 1919, he established a school in Stuttgart, Germany, near a factory. The school was called the Waldorf School. It was the first school of a movement in education, an attempt to educate the whole child. His school was the first to emphasize holism (*whole* + *ism*) in education. Steiner believed in educating the head, the heart, and the hands of a child.

Early Education

3   Even in kindergarten, every lesson has connections to other lessons. Nothing happens in a Waldorf School without thought of what it causes and how the child learns from it. Children begin to learn to read by listening to stories. For example, in kindergarten and first grade, at ages five and six, they hear fairy tales. These stories feed their imaginations. Then, at seven, when they begin to be able to reason, they hear the fables of Aesop, stories with strong moral messages. Another year passes, and they hear about famous people. These great people are models for young children to follow.

Writing

4   Learning to write is an important aspect of education. In first grade, Waldorf School children do form drawing. They practice making loops and long wavy lines and learn how to use colored pencils and chalk. They are preparing for writing. When the child is ready, the teacher introduces the letters of the alphabet. Thus the child learns the basic parts of writing. Reading comes out of the desire of the child to tell his or her own story. The children produce short tales of their own. Simple books, and then more complex ones, become part of the everyday scene at the school, and gradually the children find themselves reading without trauma or stress.

Art

5   In all the 700-plus Waldorf Schools in the world, children of six years of age learn to knit. They play with watercolors and paper and create drawings in the primary colors (yellow, blue, and red). They mold pieces of beeswax into the shapes of animals and flowers. They also learn to play simple musical instruments, such as the recorder. According to Steiner, the artist within each child is awakened. The artist loves to learn and create.

Music and Handwork

6   In these ways, the Waldorf School system is holistic. Every lesson is part of life in general. Every aspect of schooling affects some other part of the education of the child. The child knits a simple narrow strip that becomes a protective bag for the child's recorder. The recorder lessons teach about music, notes, reading music, songs, tone, sound, and a part of physics. Learning to play a recorder is also learning how to follow a discipline, a rule. Children learn to pay attention to one another because they play their recorders together. There is also room for some students to excel, to learn how to play the recorder and other musical instruments very well.

Thinking

7   Steiner believed in creative thought. He understood that children have to learn to think. And he realized the strong link between defining a problem and solving it. He knew about both creative and critical thinking, and he recognized that they are very similar processes. The adult needs to be able to observe a situation, analyze it, and then state the difficulties in the situation (critical thinking). The next step is to work out a solution to the problem (creative thinking). A child, through safe situations in school, must learn the same process. Critical thinking and creative thinking, therefore, are the basis of the Waldorf method. Teaching people to be thinking human beings is the goal of the Waldorf system.

Drama

8   In a Waldorf School, every child participates in drama. There are simple plays that even little children can act out. Children do good memory work as they learn the lines of the play. The creation of the stage set and the costumes is also part of putting on a play. Parents and teachers may help the children, but the experience is theirs alone. Furthermore, the unique personality of every child is respected. Children learn several roles, experiment with different parts of their personalities, and are free to make their own choices.

Nature

9   Experience is important in learning about Mother Earth. Therefore, every Waldorf School has a vegetable garden and a flower garden. The children learn about planting, caring for plants, and harvesting. The school will also have some farm animals. Perhaps a pair of sheep will be a third grade's responsibility. The third-graders feed the sheep, make sure there is water for them, and watch their growth. In the spring, wool on the sheep is cut for wool, and the children wash the wool and learn to brush it. The wool is used in many art projects the next year.

Reading

10   Steiner also understood the importance of reading. Reading is the foundation of all human learning. So in each grade, the children have main lesson books. These are specially made notebooks in which the children write the lessons they learn through stories. They draw pictures to illustrate the stories. They decorate their main lesson books. Textbooks as such are not the most important part of the schoolwork. The main lesson books are the textbooks, and the children write them.

Speaking

11   Another aspect of Waldorf education is a focus on learning to speak well and clearly. Through special exercises, the rhythm

of speech improves. The children learn through a kind of special dance how to experience the beauty of sounds in speech.

Philosophy

12   Steiner believed that children should learn when they are ready to learn. Children who are studying some things too early, he said, suffer from a kind of trauma. This stress and worry come from any negative experience. And children are afraid of difficult situations and shy away from them. Steiner wanted children protected from things that stop education and learning. Therefore, children should learn to read slowly and naturally. They should not have to be in a remedial reading classroom if they are not ready to learn to read.

Holism

13   Waldorf education is special in another way. Ideally, a teacher begins with a group of children in first grade and moves with them through the first eight grades. That teacher, because of eight years with a class, becomes like a special model or mentor, not unlike a parent. The teacher knows the children in his or her class family very well, and the teacher can work with parents and each child to bring out the best qualities of character. In a Waldorf School, the changing of the seasons and the holidays are all very important celebrations. Holidays like a Harvest Festival in the fall, a Winterfaire in December, and May Day in the spring add a sense of the wholeness of the year.

14   The holism of the education is real to the children. They develop into human beings who are able to develop purpose in their lives. The idea is to welcome the children into the school with a feeling of sincerity, teach them with love, and let them go in freedom.

Detail Questions

Find the answers to these questions.

1. Who started Waldorf Schools? _____

2. When did he live? _____

3. Where was this person from? _____

4. Where was the first Waldorf School? _____

5. What year was it started? _____

6. How many Waldorf Schools are there in the world?

   _____

7. What does *holism* mean? _____

8. When are holidays celebrated at the school? _____

9. When is Winterfaire? _____

10. What is the goal of Waldorf education? _____

Detail Questions: *True* or *False*?

Decide whether each statement is true or false according to the reading. Circle *true* or *false*. Also write the number of the paragraph with the answer in the reading.

1. Aesop was a teacher.   true   false   _____

2. Waldorf School children learn   true   false   _____
   to write in the first grade.

3. The first Waldorf School was in Austria.   true   false   _____

4. A Waldorf teacher usually teaches   true   false   _____
   the same children for eight years.

5. Waldorf School books are big textbooks.   true   false   _____

6. A fable is a story with a strong   true   false   _____
   message or lesson in it.

7. In a Waldorf School, the children   true   false   _____
   learn to play musical instruments.

8. In a Waldorf School, the children   true   false   _____
   have remedial reading classes.

9. Creative thinking is similar   true   false   _____
   to critical thinking.

10. A main lesson book is a textbook   true   false   _____
    made by a child.

General Comprehension

Read each question carefully. Perhaps you can answer a question without looking at the reading. It is all right to do so. Perhaps you need to look in the reading to find the answer.

1. Why should children read about famous people?

   _____

2. What do children in a Waldorf School use beeswax for?

   _____

3. When do they learn to knit? _____

4. What do children learn about physics from learning to play a musical instrument?

   _____

5. Why does every Waldorf School have a garden? _____

6. How does a child in a Waldorf School begin to learn to read?

   _____

7. What are the textbooks in a Waldorf School? _____

8. Why don't Waldorf children ever sit in a remedial reading classroom?

   _____

Opinions

Read the sentences. Check *I agree, I disagree,* or *I'm not sure.* Then work with a classmate. Do you and your classmate have the same answers? Why or why not?

1. Rudolf Steiner had some interesting ideas about education of children.

   ❏ I agree.   ❏ I disagree.   ❏ I'm not sure.

2. A child should be ready to learn to read before he or she tries to read.

   ❏ I agree.   ❏ I disagree.   ❏ I'm not sure.

3. It is good to teach young children to knit.

   ❏ I agree.   ❏ I disagree.   ❏ I'm not sure.

4. Fairy tales are good for young children's creative thinking.

   ❏ I agree.   ❏ I disagree.   ❏ I'm not sure.

5. A child should want to learn, not have to learn.

   ❏ I agree.   ❏ I disagree.   ❏ I'm not sure.

6. A school should teach lessons about life.

   ❏ I agree.   ❏ I disagree.   ❏ I'm not sure.

7. Children of seven years of age know the difference between right and wrong.

   ❏ I agree.   ❏ I disagree.   ❏ I'm not sure.

8. Children want to learn to read and write to tell their own stories.

   ❏ I agree.   ❏ I disagree.   ❏ I'm not sure.

9. Critical thinking and creative thinking are similar.

   ❏ I agree.   ❏ I disagree.   ❏ I'm not sure.

10. A teacher shouldn't stay with a class for eight years.

    ❏ I agree.   ❏ I disagree.   ❏ I'm not sure.

Main Ideas

In this list of sentences below, there is one main idea for the whole reading on Holism in Education. The rest of the sentences are the main ideas from each of the paragraphs. First find the main idea for the reading. Write *MI* in the blank in front of that sentence. Then in the blank in front of each of the other sentences, write the number of the paragraph with the answer in the reading.

1. _____ Drama is an important part of learning.

2. _____ Stories—beginning with imaginative stories, then stories with lessons, and then stories about famous people—are the beginning of learning to read and organize ideas.

3. _____ For many years there have been discussions about what and how children should learn.

4. _____ Steiner used the ideas of many great teachers and a desire to educate the whole child to start the first Waldorf School.

5. _____ Waldorf education is a holistic way of teaching children.

6. _____ A child must learn to speak clearly and well.

7. _____ Steiner wanted children to learn how to think.

8. _____ First-grade children learn how to knit, paint, and play musical instruments.

9. _____ A class should be like a family, with one teacher from grade one to grade eight.

10. _____ Steiner believed that a child becomes ready to learn and then learns naturally; forcing a child to learn before then hurts the child.

11. _____ Children need to learn about animals and farming by raising animals and gardening.

12. _____ Children make their own reading books by writing the stories they hear.

13. _____ Writing begins with drawing and develops into reading because children want to tell their stories.

14. _____ The conclusion is that Waldorf education is holistic.

15. _____ Every lesson has links to every other lesson, so that children understand that all parts of the world are connected.

Inferences

1. How long does a Waldorf education last for a child?

   a. one year

   b. eight years

   c. nine years

2. How does the study of sound begin in a Waldorf School?

   a. with a physics lesson

   b. with storytelling

   c. with learning to play a musical instrument

3. Why don't some Waldorf School children learn to read books until third grade?

   a. They don't have books.

   b. They are not ready to learn to read yet.

   c. They don't learn to read until third grade.

4. Why does form drawing come before learning to write?

   a. Form drawing is making loops and wavy lines in preparation for learning to write.

   b. Form drawing is more important than language.

   c. Form drawing is another word for writing the letters of the alphabet.

5. What do you have to do before you can solve a problem?

   a. come up with many answers to your questions

   b. define the problem

   c. learn to live with the problem

6. Observing a situation is important before one can…

   a. define it.

   b. analyze it.

   c. solve it.

📊 Vocabulary Building

Find a word from the list that means almost the same as the word in **bold**. Rewrite the sentence with the matching word.

link	form	model	analyze	discipline
tales	excel	trauma	purpose	observing

1. The sick man is in the hospital. The doctors there are **watching** his health closely.

   _____

2. The little girl was an artist in first grade. Her teachers knew that she would **do very well** in art.

   _____

3. Every school needs to have **a set of rules** for children to follow.

   _____

4. A child who tries and fails many times will have **stress and worry** about learning.

   _____

5. The best way for a child to learn is to follow a good **example**.

   _____

6. To solve a problem, I have to **study to understand** it first.

   _____

7. In a Waldorf School there is a **reason** for every kind of lesson.

   _____

8. There is a strong **connection** between thinking and imagination.

   _____

9. What is the **shape** of the first letter of the alphabet?

   _____

10. Everyone likes to tell **stories** in the evening.

📓 Vocabulary Journal

Choose five words from the Vocabulary in Context list to be your target words. Write the words here:

_____ _____ _____ _____ _____

Now write them in your vocabulary journal. Remember to include the following parts:

- your target word
- the sentence from the Main Reading in which your target word appears
- a definition, including the part of speech
- some sentences of your own

Discussion Ideas

1. In a Waldorf first grade, the children have colored pencils and paints in the primary colors (red, blue, and yellow). Why don't they have the other colors?

2. Some teachers say three things. First they say, "This is what I'm going to teach you." Then they say, "This is what I'm teaching you." And then after the lesson, they say, "This is what I taught you." What do you think? Is it good to tell children what they are learning? Is it better for them to learn naturally, without thinking about what they are learning?

3. A father took his child out of a Waldorf School after the second grade. A year later, his daughter's Waldorf teacher saw the man at a department store. She stopped to ask the man about his daughter. "Oh, she is doing much better," the man said. "We took her out of the Waldorf School because she wasn't reading yet. But after less than a month at the regular public school, she was reading at grade level." What do you think the Waldorf teacher said to this parent?

Writing Ideas

1. What stories did you like as a child? Write one of the stories that you remember.

2. Think about your own education. Did you ever experience trauma of any kind? Was there ever a time that you felt stress and worry about going to school? If so, how do you feel about it now?

Organization of Ideas

Children go through many kinds of schools before they finish education. Work with your classmates. Put these terms in order, start to finish:

_____ graduate school   _____ elementary school

_____ undergraduate college   _____ nursery school

_____ kindergarten   _____ high school

_____ middle or junior high school

Related Reading

The "News" in Education

1   Education changes with time. Because of these changes, the face of education and **access** to education are different today. The most obvious change is that there are different things to teach. In fact, there is much more to teach. Learning and research have increased greatly in the past century. Great advances in science mean that there is much more information to teach. Some of the ideas of the past were wrong, so the **content** of books is different. For example, in a beginning biology class today, more than 70% of the information that students learn today was not known twenty years ago. That's an important reason for change! As scientists learn more, there will be more for students to learn.

2   Another reason for changes in education is that there are new teaching tools. For centuries, schools had no books. The teachers gave lessons explaining ideas to students. Today teachers and students use books, including e-books. They also use technology. For example, many of them use computers, video, and **on-line communication.** There are even **electronic classrooms.** Through **interactive** instructional television **networks** (IITV), a teacher can teach students in different places. Their IITV classrooms use radio **signals** or **satellite communication** to carry the communication from tower to tower.

3   There are differences between the traditional classroom and the IITV classroom, of course. However, most of these differences are easy to **overcome**. Perhaps one student wants to have a **private** conversation with the teacher. If teacher and student talk on the IITV network, there is no **privacy**. Everyone else in the class can hear what they say. Therefore, their conversation must happen over telephone lines or through electronic mail (e-mail).

4   No one really knows how this change in students' ability to talk privately with a teacher changes the educational experience. Some students decide not to talk to the teacher because it cannot happen naturally after class. She could send an e-mail message or decide **not to bother** the teacher. This lack of personal contact with the teacher is just one **potential** problem. Another is that the students in different classroom places cannot speak with one another as easily. One solution to this drawback is the class chat room. To **facilitate** (make possible, make easier) students' conversation about a topic, the teacher can set up an Internet **chat room** or a **bulletin board**. A number of general topics are posted, and the students can write in their thoughts on the topic. Some students are **shy** of using these kinds of communication tools. Perhaps they don't have access to the equipment, or maybe they don't know how to get to a chat room on the Internet.

Communication among students is possible, but it takes place through a medium that is different from voices in a classroom.

5   On the other hand, there are great advantages to teaching though IITV. Great numbers of students can "attend" the class. Education is not limited to those who are near a university. Another advantage is the ability to show things to students. Every IITV classroom has a *padcam*™. This special camera focuses on any picture, book page, or object that the teacher wants the students to see. The camera focuses on a rectangle—the pad. A teacher can put a picture, for example, on the pad of the *padcam*™. The padcam™ has a **zoom lens**. Therefore, the teacher can focus on tiny things in the picture and make them much bigger than life. Art history teachers and anthropologists love the padcam™. They use it to make their lessons more interesting. They can show **details** with ease.

6   Computer programs such as PowerPoint® connect easily to the electronic equipment in interactive television. Therefore, the **presentation** of ideas can happen quite well. The teacher can put the main ideas on the screen, so the students know what the main ideas of the lesson are. Another advantage is the ability to include videos in lessons. It is easy to show **movies** or parts of cinemas. Furthermore, there can be a videotape record of every lesson. A student who misses a class can watch the tape. Then he knows exactly what happened in class!

7   Students change from generation to **generation**. The students of today learn in different ways from their grandparents forty years ago or their parents twenty years ago. Today's students grew up under different conditions. Most of them have always had electricity. Perhaps they have always had television. They grew up with technology. The things that a person has always known seem natural to him or her. Of course, there is always change. Changes in society happen slowly, one at a time.

Therefore, people usually accept changes as natural. For older people, the changes today seem to happen very fast. They find it more difficult to keep up with the changes. Younger students are used to a faster speed of living. They accept the speed as something natural.

8   The new technology, the change in personality of students, and the changes in content all affect education today. Schools look different, teachers do different kinds of teaching, and students learn different things. It is impossible to tell how education will change in the next generation. One cannot be sure of anything— except that it will change.

Vocabulary in Context

1. In an **interactive** television classroom, the teacher can talk to the students, and the students can talk with the teacher. They exchange information. Their conversations, or **interactions**, are the same as two people talking in the same room except for one thing. These people are talking over a great distance, and they see each other on TV screens.

   • An **interaction** is _____ .

   • An **interactive** situation is one is which _____ .

2. A **radio signal** is like a short burst of light. It travels and can be changed into video or sound. Television and radio use this kind of microwave to send information around the world.

   • A **radio signal** is _____ that can _____ .

3. A conversation between you and me (and no one else) is a **private** conversation. Only when a person is alone does he or she have true **privacy**.

   • A **private** matter is one that is _____ .

   • A person has **privacy** when he or she is _____ .

4. In a city, there are many interesting places to go and things to see. There are museums, libraries, and theaters, to name a few. A person who lives in a rural area, on a farm or in a small village, doesn't **have access to** so many interesting places. The city person has choices; he or she **is not limited** in the way that any rural person is.

- To **have access to** a place means to be able to _____ .

- To **be limited** is not to _____ .

5. On the Internet, there are places where **on-line communication** takes place. People can exchange information electronically. They log on to a **chat room** or a **bulletin board**. There they see topics to discuss. They can add their own opinions.

- A **chat room** and a **bulletin board** are places on the Internet

  where people can _____ .

- **On-line communication** happens when people _____ .

6. The Internet is a **network**. One person can connect to dozens of other people. Each of them can connect to dozens of others. Therefore, there are links in several directions, like a net.

- A **network** results from _____ .

7. We say that grandparents are the oldest **generation**, or age group. Parents are the middle generation, and their children are the youngest generation. For purpose of population study, a generation is about twenty years of history.

- A **generation** is a group of people who are _____ .

8. The **zoom lens** of a camera allows the photographer to "move close" to the subject without moving at all. The zoom lens focuses on **details** or small aspects of the subject so that a picture can show these parts.

- A **zoom lens** is a special camera part that makes it possible for a

  photographer to _____ .

- A **detail** is a _____ .

9. Some students don't feel comfortable calling a teacher on the telephone if they need help. Perhaps they **are shy about** talking to a teacher, or else they don't want to **bother** their teacher. In either case, they should know that most teachers are glad to help their students. Teachers like to feel needed, so a student should be willing to ask questions. Also, most teachers consider helping students to be part of their jobs, so asking questions isn't wasting their time!

   • To **be shy about** doing something is to be _____ .

   • To **bother someone** is to _____ .

10. A possible way to **overcome** the need for more and more education is to use electronic communication. There are not enough classrooms, and there aren't enough teachers to solve the problem of the need for education. The **potential** use of e-mail and interactive television as schoolrooms is truly unlimited. Any person with a television set can learn by watching and listening.

   • A **potential** solution is a _____ one.

   • To **overcome** a problem is to find a _____ to it.

Drawing Conclusions

1. The title shows that there are three new things in education. One of them is new content. Think about the meaning of new content. Which of the sentences in this list are true about the content of today's classrooms? Write a check (✓) in front of each one that you think is true.

   a. _____ Teachers do not know the new content.

   b. _____ There is more for teachers to know and more for teachers to teach than fifty years ago.

   c. _____ Some things that one's parents learned are not part of education today.

   d. _____ Children today have to learn more than their parents and grandparents did in school.

   e. _____ A school classroom today looks the same as a classroom in 1950.

2. A second new aspect of education is the use of new tools. Think about the changes in tools. Which of the sentences in this list about new tools are probably true? Write a check (✓) in front of each one that you think is true.

   a. _____ Most of the new educational tools are electronic in nature.

   b. _____ There are many new possibilities of ways to learn because of these new tools.

   c. _____ These new tools in education are dangerous to teachers and students.

   d. _____ One must learn to use the new tools for education.

   e. _____ An example of a new learning tool is interactive television.

3. The third of the new things in education is a new generation to teach. Think about the changes in the students. Which of the sentences in this list about new students are probably true? Write a check (✓) in front of each one that you think is true.

   a. _____ The students of today grew up in a different world.

   b. _____ The parents of today's students were probably smarter than their children.

   c. _____ All people learn the same way.

   d. _____ Today's students learn in ways that older people did not learn.

   e. _____ It is probably a good idea to teach the young and the old together.

4. Which of these statements are probably true about IITV? Write a check (✓) in front of each one that you think is true.

   a. _____ IITV is expensive.

   b. _____ IITV is easy to set up and run.

   c. _____ IITV could exist without computers.

   d. _____ IITV gives a teacher a lot of advantages.

   e. _____ IITV can help every person in every country to learn more.

5. Which of these statements are probably true about the future of education? Write a check (✓) in front of each one that you think is true.

    a. _____ Education has changed enough, so it will not change any more.

    b. _____ There will likely be new tools for education in the future.

    c. _____ Old teachers have to learn new ways to teach.

    d. _____ There will always be developments in education.

    e. _____ There is no future in education.

Discussion Ideas

1. Think about your life as a student. What items on this list are necessary for a student? Write an *X* in the blank in front of each of the needed items. Write the letter *0* in the blank in front of each unnecessary thing.

    A student needs money…

    _____ for books

    _____ for tuition

    _____ for a room to live in

    _____ for entertainment

    _____ for food

    _____ for new clothes

    _____ for movies

    _____ for school costs

Compare your list to the list of another student in the class. Do the two of you agree? Why or why not?

⏱ Timed Reading 1

Maria Montessori
(1870–1952)

In 1894 Maria Montessori became the first woman in Italy to receive a medical degree. However, she is remembered for her ideas about education, not for being a doctor. Her work with children began because she was a doctor. As director of a hospital, she became interested in children with *mental retardation.* These children were slow learners, not very intelligent. She believed that these children could learn. She gave these children ideas to think about, activities to do with their hands, and ways to feel good about themselves. And the children began to learn! Some children were in her hospital because their parents couldn't take care of them, because the children couldn't learn. But Montessori showed that they could learn! Soon her slow children passed the Italian public school test for sixth-grade students. Soon everyone in Italy knew about Dr. Maria Montessori's ideas about education.

Montessori believed that her methods would work well with children of normal intelligence, too. In 1907 she opened the first Montessori school, the Children's House, in a poor part of Rome. Observers came to see the children at this school. Before the age of five, the children had learned to read and write. They liked working more than playing. And they could focus on an activity and not get tired.

For Montessori, the adults in a school were not just teachers. They were classroom leaders and directors. Their job was to direct the interests of the children, to help them develop. A director observes a child. When the child shows signs of being ready to learn something new, the director helps the child begin.

Soon many people in other places heard about the Montessori school in Rome. And her ideas spread. However, by 1934, Maria Montessori left Italy. The government there was not friendly to her ideas. She went to Spain for two years and then to the Netherlands. In Amsterdam, she established a special school for "Montessori" teachers. Later she lived in both India and Sri Lanka. Everywhere she went, she started more Children's Houses, and her ideas of teaching children spread all over the world.

Time: _____

Now answer these questions as quickly as you can.

1. Maria Montessori was first a...
   a. teacher of children.
   b. medical doctor.
   c. child in a special hospital school.

2. Montessori's first students were...
   a. doctors.   b. teachers.   c. mentally retarded.

3. The first Montessori school was in...
   a. Amsterdam.   b. Italy.   c. Sri Lanka.

4. In a Montessori school, the adults are called…

   a. teachers.

   b. learners.

   c. directors.

5. Children with mental retardation…

   a. don't learn quickly.

   b. learn fast.

   c. usually do not learn at all.

6. Maria Montessori left Italy in…

   a. 1894.   b. 1907.   c. 1934.

7. Montessori left Italy because…

   a. of the government.

   b. the children passed the sixth-grade test of Italian public schools.

   c. she finished her work there.

8. When she left Italy, Montessori first went to live in…

   a. Sri Lanka.

   b. Spain.

   c. Amsterdam.

9. The first name for the schools that Maria Montessori started was…

   a. Montessori Schools.

   b. Children's Houses.

   c. Hospital Schools.

10. The first Montessori school for teachers was in…

    a. Italy.

    b. Spain.

    c. the Netherlands.

Timed Reading 2

Lev Semenovich Vygotsky (1896–1934)

The beginning of the 20th century was a time of great change in education. Many psychologists and philosophers were discussing learning. They were observing children to understand them better. Because of their discussions, schools, teachers' education, and curriculum all changed.

One of these people was a Russian psychologist and educator. Like another psychologist, the Swiss philosopher Jean Piaget (1896-1980), Lev Vygotsky was interested in how children learn. Like Maria Montessori in Italy and Rudolf Steiner in Germany and Austria, he turned his ideas into action. Unlike Steiner and Montessori, however, he didn't start any schools.

Vygotsky and Piaget (pee-ah-ZHEY) did not always agree. According to Piaget, for example, a child developed first. Learning followed the development. In Vygotsky's opinion, a child develops because of social interaction. The child, he said, learns everything twice. First the child copies what older and experienced people do and say. Then the child learns on an individual level, inside his or her head. A good relationship with an older person (like a parent or a teacher) helps the child learn quickly and well.

Another of Vygotsky's ideas is about when a child learns. Maria Montessori believed in a child's "sensitive period." During this time, she said, a child was ready to learn a particular skill. Steiner believed a child had to be ready to learn. To Vygotsky, this period is even more important. He said a child could learn only during this period. If a child did not learn during this period of time, the child would never learn the skill.

For this reason, Vygotsky believed in education. Only human beings are born into a history of learning. For centuries, people have been learning. A child must learn how to use the experience of the past. Hearing the stories is part of learning. Talking with other people (who know) makes the information real to a child.

Vygotsky wrote about his ideas. He taught his students about his beliefs. Fortunately, his students saved his notes. Vygotsky died very young, at the age of 38. Even so, his ideas have been very important in the history of education.

Time: _____

Now answer these questions as quickly as you can.

1. Vygotsky came from…
   a. Austria.   b. Russia.   c. Switzerland.

2. Which of these people started schools?
   a. Vygotsky and Piaget
   b. Piaget and Montessori
   c. Montessori and Steiner

3. Who believed in a "sensitive period" for learning a skill?
   a. Piaget   b. Steiner   c. Montessori

4. Who believed that development comes before learning?

   a. Piaget

   b. Vygotsky

   c. all psychologists

5. When was Vygotsky born?

   a. 1938   b. 1896   c. 1934

6. For Vygotsky, how does a child learn?

   a. from older people who know more

   b. alone, but when he or she is ready

   c. from reading

7. For Piaget, what comes first?

   a. reading

   b. development

   c. talking with other people

8. Which of these leaders in education believed in the aspect of social interaction?

   a. Piaget

   b. Montessori

   c. Vygotsky

9. Who lived in Austria and Germany?

   a. Vygotsky

   b. Montessori

   c. Steiner

10. Why do children have to learn so much?

    a. because people in the past have collected a great deal of information

    b. because old books smell bad

    c. because children are not good at learning

ON THE ROAD

 **Preparation**

Topic

What do you expect? Survey this unit. Note the photographs, pictures, and titles. The titles tell you the general topics.

Anticipation

1. This unit will be about taking trips and finding excitement. The first reading will be about traveling a great distance to many different countries. Here are some questions about travel. Discuss them with your classmates.

   a. What are some common or usual places people travel?

   b. What are some unusual places people travel?

   c. Why do people travel?

   d. What do you learn when you travel?

2. Which of the following ideas are likely to be in a reading in this unit? Write *likely* or *unlikely* in each blank.

   a. _____ People travel because they want to have fun.

   b. _____ People travel in many unusual ways.

   c. _____ There are some places that many tourists visit.

   d. _____ Bicycles are a good means of transportation.

   e. _____ Some people prefer to travel in balloons.

   f. _____ Anyone can build a boat.

3. Choose some key words for this unit. Make a list.

   _____ _____ _____

   _____ _____ _____

   _____ _____

📊 Vocabulary in Context

Find the meanings of the words in **bold** type, and write them in the blanks.

1. The young people of Athens were **impressed** by the **philosopher** Socrates. He was able to influence them well because they admired him as a wise thinker. The older people, however, did not trust the **attitudes** (ways of thinking) that he was teaching the **curious** Athenian youths. He taught them to ask questions and to answer with more questions. Many centuries later, Socrates' way of thinking has continued to influence education; many teachers ask students questions to help them find their own answers.

   • He **impressed** me. = I _____ him, and he

     _____ me.

   • A **philosopher** is a _____ .

   • An **attitude** is a _____ .

   • A **curious** person is one who _____ .

2. Socrates was a great teacher, and the youths of Athens looked up to him. They gave him **respect** and admiration.

   • When a person has the **respect** of other people, other people

     _____ .

3. The tourists went into the tourist agency with an important question. They needed to **extend** their visas for another month. Their permission to stay in the country was for six weeks only, but they wanted to stay a longer time and see more places.

   • To **extend** means _____ .

4. The words **horizon** and **horizontal** are related. The horizon is the line where the sky seems to meet the Earth. A horizontal line is one that is parallel to the horizon. It goes from side to side. A **vertical** line is **perpendicular**, or at right angles, to a horizontal line. It goes up and down, from top to bottom.

   • The **horizon** is _____ .

   • A **horizontal** line is _____ .

- A **vertical** line is _____ .

- A **perpendicular** line is _____ .

5. The train moved so swiftly through the town that only quick looks at people and buildings were possible. These **glimpses**, however, made a vivid, lively picture in the child's mind.

   - A **glimpse** is a _____ .

6. The spaceship was traveling toward the moon. The moon was the **destination**, or goal.

   - A **destination** is a _____ .

7. The **contrasts** between city life and country life are great. One important difference is that people in small towns know one another well.

   - A **contrast** is a _____ .

8. Because the early world explorers like Marco Polo, Magellan, and Columbus did not know their way, their trips were true **adventures**, or exciting and dangerous experiences. To some people, these **adventurers** were foolish because they went into unknown places. They were often in danger as a result.

   - An **adventure** is a _____ .

   - An **adventurer** is a _____ .

9. The small airplane was leaving from the airport. Suddenly some birds flew up in front of the plane. As the plane took off, the pilot was **temporarily distracted** by those birds. In other words, the birds took his attention away from the plane's controls for a short time. He almost lost control of the little plane.

   - **Temporarily** means for a _____ .

   - To be **distracted** is to _____ .

10. Most geographers agree that there are seven **continents**, or large land masses, in the world: Africa, Antarctica, Asia, Australia, Europe, North America, and South America.

    - A **continent** is a _____ .

11. Her bicycle had a flat tire, and her car needed gas. There were no buses in her neighborhood. But the woman had an important appointment. So she put on her comfortable walking shoes and began the long **trek** to town.

     - A **trek** is a _____ .

12. The blind man has a dog to lead him and help him. The two of them go everywhere and do everything together. The animal and the person are constant **companions** and close friends.

     - A **companion** is a _____ .

Main Reading

On the Road

Part 1

Traveling to Learn; Learning to Travel

1   When Mike and Susan began their journey through South America, they wanted to learn. To them, South America was a large continent full of adventure. On the map, the continent looked wide at the equator and narrow close to the Earth's southern pole in Antarctica. They had seen pictures, read books and magazines, studied the Internet, and talked to friends. They were impressed by the basic geography of the continent: the Andes Mountain Range, the Amazon River Basin, the Patagonia area of Argentina and Chile, and the altiplano of Bolivia and Peru. They were curious about the different cultures and attitudes of the people in the regions. But what would they really learn on their journey? They were not sure, but they knew they would extend their horizons and knowledge.

2   Their dream was to explore the huge continent of South America by car. They planned their trip carefully. They did not focus on their itinerary—where they would go every day. They thought the itinerary would happen naturally as they traveled. Instead, they focused on what they needed to make the trip. First they bought a good, strong car. They chose a four-wheel-drive sport-utility vehicle. This car needed to be strong and reliable to go long distances on any kind of road. Then, deciding on the equipment to carry in the car was a real challenge. They needed to be prepared for any situation.

3   Some of the equipment that they chose was unique for long-distance travelers: a laptop computer, a global positioning system (GPS), a printer, and a satellite telephone communication system. These were electronic devices to help them communicate on the trip. The satellite telephone communication system gave them the ability to communicate from almost any location. The computer enabled them to communicate by e-mail and to use CD encyclopedias for information. The GPS, by receiving signals from satellites around the Earth, gave them their exact position on a map at any time. And with the computer and the printer, they could print whatever they needed on paper. Mike and Susan felt confident that they could communicate with family, friends, and business contacts. With the GPS and maps, they would not get lost.

4   Besides all this technical equipment, Mike and Susan took many extra car parts and clothing for all kinds of conditions. They took camping gear such as a tent, sleeping bags, portable cooking equipment, and freeze-dried food. They had flashlights, candles, insect repellent, water-purification systems, and medicines. They tried to pack efficiently so the car would not be too heavy or look too full. They also had safety rules they tried to follow. They decided not to travel at night, not to pick up strangers, and

not to drive in bad weather or if they were tired. As traveling companions, they made a promise to each other to meet and talk to as many people as they could and to make each day a new adventure.

5   They began their road journey in Brazil, the largest country in Latin America. Brazil has approximately half the land and population of South America. Rio de Janeiro was the starting point. Rio is a vibrant city sitting between the Carioca Mountains and the South Atlantic Ocean. This modern, busy city is famous for white sand beaches, steep rock mountains, and green Atlantic rain forests. They left Rio at the end of October and drove into the interior of Brazil. Their destination was a large wildlife area

in the state of Matto Grosso do Sul, near the city of Campo Grande. This area is called the Pantanal. The Pantanal was a three-day drive west from Rio through the state of São Paulo.

The Pantanal

6   The Pantanal is the largest and densest wildlife area outside of Africa. Heavy rains flood this large, flat area for six months of the year. These rains create high waters. As it rains, the many rivers slowly move south into the Paraguay River. Every year, the high water brings a new full cycle of life to the swamp, or wetlands. Small snails and shrimp grow in the water, providing food for the fish. The fish then multiply and grow quickly, providing food for the alligators. The tall grasses are food for grazing animals such as capybara (the largest rodents in the world) and deer. Finally, thousands of birds eat the fish, fruit, and insects. Birds such as black toucans with large yellow bills, bright green parakeets and parrots, and pairs of large blue macaws fly across the sky. Here in the Pantanal, birds that walk in shallow water are particularly plentiful. Huge storks the size of a grown person, herons, ibises, egrets, and pink spoonbill flamencos walk slowly through the water, looking for food. Birds called kingfishers catch small fish, and black cormorants dry their wings in the sun. The plentiful food cycle makes this area very dense for wildlife.

7   While Mike and Susan were in the Pantanal, they stayed in a small hut, or house, built on poles right next to a lake. It was the dry season, so the water was low. The ponds, or pools of water, were full of jumping fish and alligators. In fact, alligators came right under their hut at night, looking for food. All day the birds called to one another. They sang, screeched, cried, and chirped. And all night insects buzzed, and frogs croaked. Mike and Susan had never experienced an environment so full of natural life. Each day they hiked, and each day they saw more wildlife. They glimpsed tortoises (land turtles), coati (small

mammals like raccoons), hawks (large hunting birds), piranha (aggressive fish), howler monkeys (monkeys that make loud, low calls in the forest), and hundreds of alligators. The abundance of wildlife and the interactions of living things deeply impressed Mike and Susan. In the five short days they spent in the Pantanal, they had learned new respect for living things.

8   They then drove south about five hours to a small town called Bonito. *Bonito* means "pretty" in Portuguese. The town of Bonito is actually not pretty, but the area around it is beautiful. The area sits on top of layers of rocks. Several rivers begin here from natural springs. The spring water pushes up through the rock layers to the rivers. The water is filtered by the rock layers as it moves upward. Therefore, the water in the rivers near the town is as clear as a glass of drinking water. The rivers are crystal clear.

9   To see these rivers, Susan and Mike joined a small group of about six other travelers to do some freshwater river snorkeling. To get to the river, they walked on a path for about 30 minutes through the forest. They walked with the group in a single line through the jungle. Suddenly, a herd of wild pigs, perhaps 50 or 60, crossed the path ahead and behind them, squealing, clacking, and grunting as they ran. The group of tourists, including Susan and Mike, were frightened by the wild pigs. Some female pigs were protecting their babies, and some large males made loud and sharp clacking noises as they ran. The people at the front and back of the group clapped their hands together to distract the wild pigs temporarily, to scare them away. Luckily, the wild pigs ran in a different direction, and everyone in the group relaxed. After several more minutes of walking, they finally arrived at the source of the river.

10   Rio da Prata was as clear as water in an aquarium. They could easily see the green underwater plants growing in the white sand. Many sizes and colors of freshwater fish—golden, green, yellow,

and red—swam slowly in the water. Mike and Susan put on their snorkeling equipment and swam with these fish for nearly three hours. They floated on the river current, and the fish swam right beside them. They were amazed that they could float down a river in the jungle. They watched the silent fish swim slowly by; at the same time, they heard the bird cries of the jungle. The contrast between the quiet of the underwater life and the noise in the jungle overhead was amazing. As they were floating down the beautiful river, a long, thick snake moved through the water. It was an anaconda, a dangerous water boa constrictor! But the snake wasn't interested in them. Finally they climbed onto the side of the river. They were cold and wet, but very happy. They were amazed that they could swim so close to wild fish. Once again, they felt the wonder of nature.

The Iguazu Falls

11   After four days exploring the waters around Bonita, Mike and Susan continued their journey south. They drove southeast for two days to one of the greatest natural wonders on Earth: the Iguazu Falls. The Iguazu River flows across a large plateau before it reaches these falls. As the Iguazu moves across the large flat land area, 30 rivers flow into it. It is a huge river by the time it reaches the cliffs at the edge of the plateau. These cliffs are three kilometers wide. There is a perpendicular drop of 90 meters to the land below. The water roars as it falls the 90 meters at a rate of 1,750 cubic meters a second. The white mist from the falling water and the light from the sun create never-ending rainbows. Visitors can see and feel the power of these waterfalls as the water drops through the green jungle to the river far below.

12   The north side of the falls is in Brazil, and the south side is in Argentina. Susan and Mike spent two days hiking on both sides of the falls—four days total. Once again, birds were everywhere. There were more toucans with their oversized bills, colorful

parrots, and swallows, small black–and–white birds, flying in and out of the falls. The many brightly colored butterflies softly flew about, landing wherever the wind and spray took them. The water fell onto rocks with green ferns, colorful orchids, and trees. Again, the beauty and power of the forces of nature impressed Susan and Mike.

Part 2

13   After four days of hiking around Iguazu Falls, Mike and Susan left Brazil. They crossed the border into Argentina and continued south. The language was Spanish for the rest of their trip. They reached Buenos Aires in five days, stopping at various places along the way. Buenos Aires, the Paris of South America, is one of the great urban centers of South America. Its means "good winds." It refers to the strong winds that brought sailors across the Atlantic Ocean to that port. Mike and Susan were impressed with the beauty of the European architecture and the carefully planned city. After three days of visiting museums and going to the theater, they continued to move south.

Patagonia

14   They drove into the great pampas of Argentina—rich fields of high grass. Then, at about 39 degrees latitude, they entered Patagonia. Patagonia is an enormous area of Argentina—about one-third of the country. It stretches all the way to the southern tip of the continent. It is a treeless plateau, a cool, dry desert. Frequent strong winds blow from the west. On this trip they drove for days through the unchanging landscape of Patagonia.

15   After driving for two days in Patagonia, they arrived at the Valdez Peninsula on the South Atlantic coast. They reached the Valdez Peninsula on November 23. This was the first place they encountered a guanaco, an animal related to the llama and the camel. Guanacos wander throughout the southern part of South America. The Valdez Peninsula was also alive with marine life: sea lions, elephant seals, whales, porpoises, and penguins. Susan and Mike spent several days watching the families of sea lions and waiting to see if the famous black-and-white orca whales would arrive. The orcas never arrived, so the adventurers continued south.

16   They drove south toward the tip of the continent, Tierra del Fuego. Four days later, on December 1, they reached the Magellan Strait. It was now summer, and the weather was pleasant. They crossed the Magellan Strait by ferryboat to the large island of Tierra del Fuego. They continued south toward the town of Ushuaia and the end of the road. The land was still gray, treeless, and windswept. Finally, they began to see a few trees, then forests, mountains, and lakes. Driving toward Ushuaia was like seeing a green oasis after many days in the desert. The sight of the southern forest, the blue-green water of the Beagle Channel, and the mountains with high white peaks was wonderful and refreshing. The port of Ushuaia, also called "World's End," is the place that many ships leave for Antarctica. Susan and Mike had talked about finding a ship for Antarctica but, in the end, decided

not to. Instead they were happy to hike and trek in the forests of the area. Just beyond the town of Ushuaia, they drove to the end of the road in South America, to a place called Lapataia Bay. The sign there read "17,848 kilometers to Alaska"—a long way to the other end of the road. After resting for four days, they changed direction and began traveling north.

Glaciers

17   The next destination was a national park in southern Chile called "Torres del Paine," near the city Punta Arenas. This park has granite towers (*torres* in Spanish) that rise vertically from milky-blue lakes. These lakes are whitish-blue because the water in them comes from melting ice under glaciers. The dramatic, snow-covered towers, or peaks, seem to come straight up from the glacier-fed lakes. Three glaciers flow from the southern part of one of the largest ice fields on Earth: the Patagonia Icecap. Susan and Mike made a seven-day trek around the towers. They were particularly impressed by the glaciers and lakes.

18   The glaciers were white-blue, sometimes deep blue. Some of the ice is hundreds of years old. The older the ice is, the bluer it is. It becomes blue because of the pressure from the weight of the

glacier above it. To their amazement, Susan and Mike discovered that glaciers make sounds: they groan, snap, and slide. Slowly large pieces of old ice break off from the glacier's edge and fall into the lake with a crash. The piece of ice then becomes an iceberg, alone in the water. The glacier actually seems to be alive as it flows slowly down from the ice fields. Mike and Susan watched and listened for hours. They felt small and unimportant in front of this powerful force of nature.

19   Their trip to this point had changed them—it taught them to notice, respect, and accept life in all ways, and the forces of nature in all forms. They had many more places to visit: other parts of Chile and Argentina, Bolivia, Peru, Ecuador, Panama, Costa Rica, Nicaragua, El Salvador, Honduras, Guatemala, Belize, and Mexico. They clearly had much more to learn. Yet, they had changed. They had begun this trip as adventurers and were becoming philosophers. They were achieving their goal of traveling to learn and learning to travel. They had completed their "U-turn." Now they were heading north, with six months and 23,000 kilometers more to travel.

Detail Questions: *True* or *False*?

Decide whether each statement is true or false according to the reading. Circle *true* or *false*. Also write the number of the paragraph with the answer in the reading.

Part 1

1. Mike and Susan explored South America by motorcycle.   true   false   _____

2. They planned their journey carefully.   true   false   _____

3. They took a computer with them.   true   false   _____

4. They had a hard time communicating with family and friends while they were on the road.   true   false   _____

5. They began their trip in Rio de Janeiro.   true   false   _____

6. They saw many animals and birds in the Pantanal.   true   false   _____

7. The town of Bonito is very pretty.   true   false   _____

8. The water in the Rio da Prata is brown.   true   false   _____

9. The Iguazu Falls are in both Brazil and Argentina.   true   false   _____

Part 2

10. Buenos Aires is sometimes called the "Athens" of South America.   true   false   _____

11. Patagonia is the name of a town in central Argentina.   true   false   _____

12. Mike and Susan took a ship from Ushuaia to Antarctica.   true   false   _____

13. The ice in glaciers is blue because the water is pure.   true   false   _____

14. According to the sign posted in Lapataia Bay, it is 23,000 km from that point

to the end of the road in Alaska.

15. Mike and Susan also planned to travel   true   false   _____
through much of Central America (Panama,
Costa Rica, Nicaragua, El Salvador,
Honduras, Guatemala, and Mexico).

Detail Questions

Skim and scan to find the answers to these questions.

1. Where did the adventurers see wild pigs? _____

2. How many wild pigs did they see? _____

3. How did they distract the wild pigs? _____

4. What kind of snake did they see in the water? _____

5. How high is Iguazu Falls? _____

6. What does *Buenos Aires* mean? _____

7. Where does the pampas begin? _____

8. What is a guanaco? _____

9. What is an orca? _____

10. Where is "World's End"? _____

General Comprehension

Read each question carefully. Perhaps you can answer a question without looking at the reading. Perhaps you need to look in the reading to find the answer. If so, then read quickly—just to find the answer. The numbers in parentheses are paragraph numbers. They show where to look for the answers.

1. Why did Mike and Susan want to travel through South America? (1, 19)

_____

_____

2. What electronic devices did they take with them? (3)

   _____

   _____

3. What were some of their safety rules? (4)

   _____

   _____

4. Why is the Pantanal full of wildlife? (6)

   _____

   _____

5. What makes the river waters near Bonito so clear? (8)

   _____

   _____

6. Answer these questions about the Iguazu Falls. (11)

   a. How many rivers flow into the Iguazu River? _____

   b. How wide are the cliffs under the falls? _____

   c. How far does the water fall? _____

   d. How much water falls each second? _____

7. What two languages, besides English, did Mike and Susan use on the trip? (8, 13)

   _____

8. Why was driving toward the town of Ushuaia like "seeing an oasis after many days in the desert"? (16)

   _____

   _____

9. What makes the ice in glaciers blue? (18)

_____

_____

10. What did they learn from their trip? (19)

_____

_____

Opinions

Read each sentence and check *I agree, I disagree,* or *I'm not sure.*

1. They did not need to have so much communication equipment.
   ❏ I agree   ❏ I disagree   ❏ I'm not sure.

2. The most dangerous part of their trip was driving in a car every day.
   ❏ I agree   ❏ I disagree   ❏ I'm not sure.

3. The world needs more large wildlife areas like the Pantanal.
   ❏ I agree   ❏ I disagree   ❏ I'm not sure.

4. Nature is fragile and needs to be protected.
   ❏ I agree   ❏ I disagree   ❏ I'm not sure.

5. Mike and Susan were better people after this trip.
   ❏ I agree   ❏ I disagree   ❏ I'm not sure.

📊 Vocabulary Building

Practice with these words and learn more about them. Circle the letter in front of the word that means almost the same as the <u>underlined</u> word. The paragraph numbers will help you.

1. The travelers noticed the <u>contrast</u> between the quiet life underwater and the noisy bird life above them. (10)

   a. similarity

   b. difference

   c. aquarium

2. The travelers <u>were curious about</u> the cultures of the people in South America. (1)

   a. wanted to know more about

   b. were part of

   c. were not interested in

3. They knew that they would <u>extend</u> their <u>horizons</u> and knowledge. (1)

   In this sentence, <u>extend</u> means...

   a. make shorter.

   b. make broader.

   c. stay the same.

   In this sentence, <u>horizon</u> means...

   a. the line where the sky meets the Earth.

   b. their physical strength.

   c. their understanding of life.

4. At the end of their long trip, they were <u>philosophers</u>. (19) In other words, they...

   a. made a long trip.

   b. had an exciting adventure.

   c. thought more about life, culture, and ideas.

Vocabulary Journal

Choose five words from the Vocabulary in Context list to be your target words. Write the words here:

_____ _____ _____ _____ _____

Now write them in your Vocabulary Journal. Remember to include the following parts:
- your target word
- the sentence from the Main Reading in which your target word appears
- a definition, including the part of speech
- some sentences of your own

Main Ideas

Read each of the following questions and circle the letter of the correct answer.

1. The main idea of paragraph 3 is that…
   a. they took many electronic devices to help them communicate.
   b. the GPS, or global positioning system, kept them from getting lost.
   c. they communicated by e-mail and used encyclopedias on CD for information.
   d. they got lost and found in one day.

2. The main idea of paragraph 6 is that…
   a. the Pantanal is an area full of many kinds of wildlife.
   b. Brazil has many different kinds of animals and birds.
   c. floods every year create a new cycle of life in the Pantanal.
   d. A plentiful food cycle makes the Pantanal full of wildlife.

3. The main idea of paragraph 10 is that…
   a. swimming close to wild fish was a wonderful feeling.
   b. the water in Rio da Prata was as clear as an aquarium.
   c. they could see a dangerous snake called a boa constrictor.
   d. they learned how to swim in a river.

4. What is the main idea of paragraph 9?

_____

5. What is the main idea of paragraph 11?

_____

6. What is the main idea of paragraph 13?

_____

7. What is the main idea of paragraph 15?

_____

8. What is the main idea of paragraph 16?

_____

9. What is the main idea of paragraph 17?

_____

Vocabulary Building

Working with Geographical Words

This reading has many words that refer to geographical sites (places) and features, such as bodies of water and large land areas. Some of these words are below. Write the letter of the best definition in the blank. The numbers in parentheses are paragraph numbers. (Note: One definition can be used twice.)

_____   1. swamp (6)

_____   2. pond (7)

_____   3. spring (8)

_____   4. falls (11)

_____   5. plateau (11, 14)

_____   6. pampas (14)

_____   7. peninsula (15)

_____   8. oasis (16)

_____   9. strait (16)

_____   10. channel (16)

a. a piece of land surrounded on three sides by water

b. a green area in the middle of a dry desert

c. narrow passage of water that connects two bodies of water

d. water coming from the ground

e. large, high, flat land area

f. rich field of high grass

g. pool of water

h. waterfall

i. wetlands

◳ **Vocabulary Building**

Categorizing Words

This reading has many specific words naming birds, mammals, fish, and reptiles. Read each word in the list below and decide if the word is a bird, a mammal, a fish, or a reptile. Then write it under the general category. The numbers in parentheses are paragraph numbers.

alligators (6)	hawks (7)	boa constrictor (10)
deer (6)	storks (6)	porpoises (15)
piranha (7)	parakeets (6)	capybara (6)
tortoises (7)	parrots (6)	guanacos (15)
sea lions (15)	whales (15)	penguins (15)
coati (7)	wild pigs (9)	swallows (12)
monkeys (7)	egrets (6)	

BIRD

_____

_____

_____

_____

_____

_____

MAMMAL

_____

_____

_____

_____

_____

FISH

_____

_____

_____

_____

_____

REPTILE

_____

_____

_____

_____

Vocabulary Building

Recognizing Action Verbs

All the verbs below are words describing sounds. Decide which ones can be used to describe possible sounds for the animals and things below. Write your answers in the blanks.

call	chirp	clack	groan
sing	snap	grunt	squeal
howl	buzz	croak	screech

1. Birds _____

2. Insects _____

3. Monkeys _____

4. Pigs _____

5. Frogs _____

6. Glaciers _____

Organization of Ideas

Focus on Reading a Map

Use the information in the reading and the map to answer these questions.

1. In which direction were Mike and Susan traveling when they began their trip in Rio de Janeiro?

   a. south   c. west

   b. southeast   d. east

2. In the part of the trip described in the reading, Mike and Susan were driving mainly…

   a. south   c. west

   b. southeast   d. east

3. In the part of the trip in the reading, in what order did they cross international borders?

   a. Brazil, Chile, Argentina, Chile

   b. Brazil, Argentina, Chile, Argentina, Chile

   c. Brazil, Uruguay, Argentina, Chile

   d. Brazil, Argentina, Chile

4. They were at the farthest point they could drive when they were at...

   a. Ushuaia.   c. the Valdez Peninsula.

   b. Punta Arenas.   d. Bonito.

5. At 39 degrees latitude south, Mike and Susan crossed into an area called...

   a. the Pantanal.   c. Patagonia.

   b. the pampas.   d. the Andes.

6. To get to Tierra del Fuego, Mike and Susan crossed a body of water called...

   a. the South Atlantic Ocean.   c. the Magellan Strait.

   b. the Paraguay River.   d. Rio de Janeiro.

7. Look at page 141. Use the map of the southern part of South America to complete this task.

   Follow the route Mike and Susan took. Draw a line between the places below in the order of their trip. You may need to look back at the reading.

Rio de Janeiro → Campo Grande → Bonito → Iguazu Falls → Buenos Aires → 39 degrees latitude → Valdez Peninsula → Ushuaia → Punta Arenas

Inferences

Read this passage about bicycles. Then read the sentences after the reading.

Bike to Work, Bike to Play

The bicycle has gone through one full circle of development already. It began as a toy for rich people. Then it was a means of transportation. Next it became a toy again. Now the bicycle is becoming popular as a means of transportation once more.

There are several reasons for the new popularity of bicycles. The cost of fuel for cars is one reason. Another is the need to keep the environment clean. The third reason is a desire for exercise. Americans are one group of people who are leaving their cars at home. In fact, for about thirty years bicycles have been outselling cars. There are more than a hundred million in the United States alone.

An institute called World Watch made a study about the future of the automobile. The researchers stated, "The automobile is much less convenient than the bicycle, and the bicycle saves more energy."

Furthermore, it is nearly as fast as the automobile for short city trips. Many people, however, are still using their cars. Why? Time is one reason. Moreover, it is still faster to drive a car than to ride a bicycle. Another reason people do not ride bikes is their lack of confidence. Some new bicycle riders do not trust themselves. If they are not completely certain that they can ride well enough, they decide to take their cars. New bicycle riders might be afraid of hurting themselves. At least in a car, there is steel around the driver.

A more important reason is lack of knowledge about the vehicle. For example, the average person does not know how to shift gears on a ten-speed bicycle. One startling bit of information indicates the cyclists' ignorance. Bicycle manufacturers have looked at the statistics about bicycle use. They say that 80% of the ten-speed bikes in the United States have never been shifted! If bike riders knew how to ride their bikes correctly, they would probably make better use of them.

Can we make these inferences? Do you think that there is enough information in the reading? Circle your answers.

1. Today the bicycle is an important means of transportation.
   a. enough information   b. not enough information

2. There are three main reasons for the increase in the bicycle's popularity.
   a. enough information   b. not enough information

3. About a million bicycles are sold in the United States alone.
   a. enough information   b. not enough information

4. John Turner belongs to World Watch. He believes in World Watch ideas. The organization prefers the bicycle to the automobile. So John seldom uses his car.
   a. enough information   b. not enough information

5. A person saves time by driving.
   a. enough information   b. not enough information

6. For short city trips, a bicycle can be faster than a car.
   a. enough information   b. not enough information

Discussion Ideas

Discuss these concepts. What are your opinions?

All over the world, students pack their possessions in a backpack and "hit the road." What reasons do they have for wanting to travel? What choices do they have to make? Would you want to make such a trip? What are the dangers? What are the benefits?

Writing Ideas

1. Traveling is a great way to learn. Do you believe it? Why or why not?
2. Write about some of your experiences in traveling.

 Timed Reading 1

Incredible Discoveries

Sometimes people find really wonderful things when they are not looking for them. We say they "discover" natural wonders. One clear example was John Colter. Colter was a mountain man who lived alone in the Rocky Mountains of the United States. He loved to walk in the mountains, but one day in 1803 he saw a strange sight. Water was shooting high into the air and falling into a pool of green water. It was a geyser, a natural water fountain. He found other pools of blue water. Some of the pools were hot. The chemicals in the water made a beautiful color, but they also made it smell bad. Nearby there were also large clear lakes and spectacular waterfalls on cold, clear mountain rivers. Colter was excited, so he told others about the place. However, the other people did not believe him. They thought that he was a dreamer; they called him a fool. After they saw these wonders, they, too, were excited. Today we call Colter's discovery Yellowstone Park.

Another example of a discoverer was Johnny Angel. In 1935, he was flying a small plane in Venezuela. His trip took him over the high mountains, where people like him were looking for gold. Angel did not find gold, but suddenly he saw an amazing sight, a waterfall. The water fell a long way down the mountain. Later he told people about this discovery, the waterfall. They came to see the spectacular sight, and they named it after Johnny—Angel Falls. It is the highest waterfall on the Earth. The water falls nearly a kilometer—979 meters, or 3,212 feet.

Johnny Angel and John Colter are called discoverers of these natural wonders. But are they? Other people lived near these places, and they knew about the pools, waterfalls, geysers, and lakes. Weren't these people the real discoverers of these extraordinary places? Perhaps these places were ordinary to them.

Colter and Angel talked about the natural wonders of the Rocky Mountains and the Venezuelan wilderness. And after that, the people from all over the Earth wanted to see them.

Time: _____

Now answer the questions as quickly as you can.

1. John Colter...
   a. lived in Venezuela.   c. saw Angel Falls.
   b. hunted for gold.   d. was a mountain man.

2. A geyser is...
   a. a waterfall.   c. a natural water fountain.
   b. a large clear lake.   d. a pool of green water.

3. After Colter talked about the geysers, people...
   a. believed his story.   c. hunted for gold.
   b. called him a fool.   d. walked in the mountains.

4. Yellowstone Park...
   a. was in Venezuela.   c. is in the Rocky Mountains.
   b. is nearly a kilometer.   d. was discovered by Johnny Colter.

5. Johnny Angel...
   a. was a mountain man.   c. lived in the Rocky Mountains.
   b. saw geysers.   d. flew a plane in Venezuela.

6. Angel Falls is...
   a. a geyser.   c. the world's highest waterfall.
   b. a spectacular lake.   d. a high mountain.

7. Johnny Angel...
   a. did not find gold.   c. loved to walk in the mountains.
   b. was a dreamer.   d. lived alone in the Rocky Mountains.

8. In ____ , John Colter discovered Yellowstone Park.
   a. 1935   c. 1803
   b. 1903   d. 1835

9. Johnny Angel saw Angel Falls in...
   a. 1835.   c. 1903.
   b. 1803.   d. 1935.

10. The main idea of the reading:

    a. John Colter discovered Yellowstone.

    b. Johnny Angel discovered Angel Falls.

    c. Angel Falls is almost a kilometer high.

    d. Wonders are there for people to discover.

🕐 Timed Reading 2

The Iditarod

In 1925 in the seaside city of Nome, Alaska, there was a terrible disaster. Nome is in the far north of Alaska. It is isolated from other cities. There were no railroads, highways, or airplanes. It was difficult to travel to Nome. In the winter, there is lots of snow, and it is very cold. In 1925, a doctor discovered that some of the people were sick with a disease called diphtheria. There was no serum for diphtheria in Nome. He could not vaccinate the people. In the city of Anchorage, people heard about the problem and sent the serum to the doctor. First the medicine was carried on the train to the small town of Tanana. Then the serum was wrapped in fur to protect it from the cold. It went by dogsled across the frozen land. It took 170 hours for the serum to reach Nome. Nine teams of dogs pulled the sled at different times. One of the men who drove the sled was Leonhard Seppala. The serum reached Nome in time to save the lives of many people. When people heard about this race to save lives, they decided to have another race. Two people who wanted to start the race again were Leonhard Seppala and his wife. In 1967 they began a race that is called the

Iditarod. In this race, dog teams pull sleds. Their drivers, called mushers, run behind the sled or ride on it. The race is from Anchorage to Nome. The distance is 1,159 miles, or 1,932 kilometers. The race takes about eleven days. Many mushers and their dogs start the race, but only a few finish it.

Mushers take very good care of their dogs because they want to win. Healthy dogs are an important part of winning the last great race. The race goes through valleys and over mountains. It crosses frozen rivers. Sometimes snow and high winds cause problems. Women as well as men are mushers. In fact, a woman named Susan Butcher has won the race. Because of a historical event, today the challenging Iditarod is part of Alaskan culture.

Time: _____

Now answer these questions as quickly as you can.

1. Nome…
   a. is the beginning of the Iditarod.
   b. is a city in Alaska.
   c. is high in the mountains.

2. A musher is…
   a. a dog team.
   b. a kind of serum.
   c. a dogsled driver.

3. Susan Butcher…
   a. is the wife of Leonhard Seppala.
   b. won the Iditarod.
   c. lives in Nome.

4. In 1925, people in Nome…

    a. had the serum that they needed.

    b. had the disease diphtheria.

    c. went to Anchorage to live.

5. One of the mushers who carried the serum in 1925 was…

    a. Tanana.   b. Susan Butcher.   c. Leonhard Seppala.

6. The serum was carried to Nome by…

    a. railroad and airplane.

    b. railroad and dogsled.

    c. dogsled and mushers.

7. The race to carry the serum took…

    a. more than 10 days.

    b. about 100 hours.

    c. 170 hours.

8. The weather during the Iditarod is usually…

    a. warm, sunny, and dry.

    b. cold with rain.

    c. cold with snow and wind.

9. The distance between Anchorage and Nome is…

    a. 170 miles.   b. 1,159 miles.   c. 1,925 miles.

10. The main idea of the passage:

    a. The Iditarod is a dogsled race across frozen rivers and mountains.

    b. The Iditarod is a dogsled race from Anchorage to Nome.

    c. The Iditarod began because of a historical event.

THE
VIRTUAL
SHOPPING
MALL

Preparation

Survey this whole unit. Think about the unit title and the other titles. Guess what this unit is about.

Topic

This unit has a main article, two related readings, and two timed readings. What are their titles? What are some of the key words in this unit? Choose five words:

_____ _____ _____ _____ _____

Anticipation

1. On a piece of paper, make a list of the things that you bought last week. Which of these things did you need to buy? Draw a circle around each of the necessary things. Which of these things did you want to buy but didn't really need? Put a check (✓) next to each of them. Where (what places) did the things that you bought come from? Which stores did you go to? Where else did you buy from (if not a store)?

2. Analyze the things in the following list. Some of them are necessary for a person to buy, and other things might be nice to have but are not necessary. In the blank, write *N* next to the necessary things, *W* next to the things that you might want, and *O* next to things that you do not want.

_____ rice	_____ perfume	_____ razor blades
_____ food	_____ a bicycle	_____ a bar of soap
_____ shoes	_____ CD player	_____ chewing gum
_____ socks	_____ toothpaste	_____ a color TV set
_____ books	_____ a computer	_____ an alarm clock
_____ a radio	_____ a telephone	_____ a winter jacket
_____ a VCR	_____ a newspaper	_____ an electronic dictionary

Vocabulary in Context

Find the meanings of the words in **bold** type, and write them in the blanks. Or figure out the meanings by looking at the context.

1. The maker of a new perfume had a successful **advertising** plan. There were **advertisements** on television and on the radio, and in magazines and on the Internet there were pictures and information. These announcements about the new **product** made everyone think about buying some. The **purpose** for advertising is to make people want to buy. There is really no other reason for it but to **persuade** people to try a product.

    a. **Advertising** and **advertisements** refer to _____ .

    b. A **purpose** is a _____ for doing something.

    c. In this example, the manufacturer's **product** is _____ .

    d. If a person wants to try a new product because of the advertising, then the advertisement persuaded the person to buy it. To **persuade** means to _____ .

2. A **manufacturer** makes a product. A **consumer** uses a product or services. A **purchaser** spends money to buy a product or services. Leticia Tellez buys a handmade sweater for her daughter Amelia. There is a label in it: Handmade by Anna Martin.

    a. _____ is the manufacturer.

    b. _____ is the purchaser.

    c. _____ is the consumer.

3. The math problem was difficult for the students to **analyze**. They had a hard time separating the problem into parts so that they could completely understand it. There was nothing **obvious** about the problem until they finished it. Then they could understand it very well—and they were surprised that it was not easy at the beginning!

    a. To **analyze** means to_____ .

    b. If something is **obvious**, then it is_____ .

4. Even though the man was tired, his thinking was still logical and clear. He made good choices in the plans for his family. His **decisions** were wise and **rational**.

   a. **Decisions** are _____ .

   b. If a person is **rational**, then his or her thinking is _____ .

5. The mother bird left her babies **vulnerable**, unprotected in their nest. If a person is **vulnerable**, he or she is _____ .

6. At holiday time in the city, large stores have beautiful window **displays** of pretty clothes and fine gifts. These **attractive** windows bring many customers into the stores—where there are large colorful metal **racks** of hats and gloves, books, and pen-and-pencil sets. The store managers work hard to arrange these shelves and frames to show the articles in a nice way.

   a. If something is **attractive**, then it is _____ .

   b. The purpose of a **display** is to _____ .

   c. A **rack** is _____ .

7. The two young athletes have **competed** with each other many times. In each race and each game they tried very hard to win. This **competition**, however, did not keep them from being friends. Each of them tried to win over the other, but they were still friends. Being on opposite teams or on different sides in a game did not hurt their friendship.

   a. To **compete** with someone means to _____ .

   b. A **competition** is _____ .

8. Television **informs** us and **influences** us. For instance, we get information about the rest of the world through television, but television also forms our opinions—through advertising and the way that news reporters report the news.

   a. To **inform** is to _____ .

   b. To **influence** someone is to _____ .

📖 **Main Reading**

The Virtual Shopping Mall

1   People buy things, items, for different reasons. They buy the products because they need them or just because they want them. People go shopping: they look around at different stores to find good deals. They "comparison-shop." In other words, they look at the same product in several stores or from several manufacturers. Then they choose to purchase the best products for themselves—their favorite ones or the ones with the lowest prices. However, many people shop because they enjoy shopping. They like to walk through stores looking at products. They think about the products, and sometimes they buy them. Today shoppers have many ways that they can go shopping.

2   People used to go to the local market to do their shopping. They went from store to store to find the products that they wanted or needed. At the meat market, customers bought meat, and at the bakery, they purchased bread. At the department store, consumers looked at the attractive displays in the windows and on the racks. They bought television sets and VCRs at the appliance store. Shoppers went from store to store comparing the products and the prices. Then they made their decisions, and they bought items. They shopped for other products in other stores, such as grocery stores, pharmacies (drugstores), hardware stores, or flower shops. The owners of the stores advertised their products to compete for business. In small towns, shoppers may still shop this way.

3   Now, however, shoppers have several choices when they want to purchase products. They may go to the shopping mall, where there are many stores in the same place under the same roof.

They can park their cars in the large parking lot and do all their shopping in one stop. Also, they probably study newspaper advertisements in the morning before they go to the mall. The ads inform them about special sales, or bargains. In the newspaper, sometimes these shoppers find discount coupons for special sales. They are ready to make rational decisions about their purchases. The shopping mall is very convenient for many people. On the other hand, other consumers shop by mail. They get catalogs and advertising flyers from manufacturers in their mailboxes. At home, they look at the displays of items on the pages in the catalogs. The catalogs show colorful pictures of the products. There are also written descriptions of the items. These descriptions tell the buyer about the materials in the product, the sizes, the colors, and the prices. The consumers analyze the products and make decisions. Then they mail their orders to the manufacturer, or they use the telephone to place their orders. Shopping by catalog is another convenient way for the consumer to go shopping.

4   Modern technology has added other ways for people to shop. Shoppers can now shop for products and services from their homes. On their television sets, viewers can choose a shopping channel. These channels are like catalogs on TV. For example, shoppers see models wearing the clothes or jewelry. They can watch a salesperson demonstrate a video camera. Or they can see a salesperson cook a meal on a special kind of kitchen appliance. The products seem to come alive and be real, not just pictures on a page in a catalog. It is easy to purchase the items. The buyers order the items by calling a number on the telephone and giving their credit card numbers. Sometimes the buyer can pay for the item in several payments (installments). The business sends the product to the consumer through the mail. Many buyers are vulnerable because it is so easy to shop this way. They use their credit cards quickly, and soon they have large bills to pay.

5   Another way shoppers use technology is on their computers. They use e-commerce. Using a computer, they shop for products and services across the country and around the world. People use computers to help them keep track of their money. For example, they do their banking and keep track of their investments. They can analyze their own financial, or money, situations. Other people pay their bills in this way. They do not write checks and mail them. Another example of e-commerce is making travel arrangements. When travelers want to go on a trip, they make their airplane and hotel reservations by using the Internet. They search the Internet for the best prices and the most convenient times for their travel. After they have analyzed the prices and times, they make their decisions. By computer, they make the reservations for their flights. The traveler can also make hotel reservations and reserve rental cars in a distant city. It is obvious that traveling is much more convenient now because of the computer.

6   Shoppers also use the Internet to find products that they want to buy. For example, a shopper who wants a new car can shop with his computer. He sees displays of many kinds of cars. He sees the colors and the equipment of the cars. He can compare the styles of the cars. Furthermore, he can learn about the prices from different car dealers. The car dealers want his business. They are in competition with one another. Therefore, they offer good prices. The buyer analyzes the information and makes his choice. Using his computer, he makes a bid, the amount of money he wants to pay for the car. Then the seller can accept his price, the bid. Or the dealer can refuse it. If the dealer refuses his bid, the shopper can search for a bargain somewhere else without leaving his home. Other purchasers are readers. They buy books on–line. They can find the titles of books that are difficult to find in the bookstores in their own city. They compare prices from several sellers. Then they make an order, they pay the cost

by using their credit cards, and the bookseller sends the books to them by mail.

7   Other people who want special products search the Internet to find those objects. Buyers can find anything on the Internet. Not only big companies and manufacturers sell products on the Internet. Anybody who has things to sell can advertise the items on the Internet. People may sell old things, antiques. People who collect antiques search the Internet. They sometimes find bargains. Art collectors buy paintings and other artwork. Other people who make things like baskets or quilts or other crafts advertise and sell their products on-line. The Internet is a huge shopping mall for anybody to buy and sell.

8   However, there are problems with buying on-line. One of those problems is that the buyer has to pay the shipping cost for the item. Sometimes this cost is high. If a buyer is not satisfied with the product, he has to pay the cost of mailing it back to the seller. Another problem is using credit cards. Usually buyers pay with their credit cards. They charge the cost on their credit card accounts. When they put their credit card numbers on the Internet to pay for the item, sometimes their numbers might be stolen. Then the thief uses the numbers to buy items. The bill for the stolen items comes to the credit card owner. Many people feel vulnerable when they put credit card numbers on the Internet. Privacy for the credit card numbers of the buyers is a problem, but manufacturers and computer experts are working to solve it. Another problem is that sometimes sellers are not honest. The items they advertise are not as good as the items on display, and their advertisements make false promises. When the buyer buys a bad product, he cannot find the dishonest seller to return the faulty item. He has lost his money. Nevertheless, although there are some problems with buying on-line, the Internet has become an important part of the international shopping mall.

Detail Questions: *True* or *False*?

Decide whether each statement is true or false according to the reading. Circle *true* or *false*. Write the number of the paragraph in the reading that shows the answer.

1. Shoppers buy bread at a bakery.　　　true　false　_____

2. Consumers use products.　　　true　false　_____

3. Purchasers compete.　　　true　false　_____

4. Manufacturers do comparison-shopping.　　　true　false　_____

5. In small towns, shoppers do not use computers or televisions. They always shop in stores.　　　true　false　_____

6. Some shoppers use catalogs instead of going to the mall to make their purchases.　　　true　false　_____

7. Using technology is an easy way to shop.　　　true　false　_____

8. E-commerce uses modern technology.　　　true　false　_____

9. Only large companies and businesses use the Internet to do business.　　　true　false　_____

10. Some businessmen are dishonest.　　　true　false　_____

General Comprehension

Try to answer the questions without looking at the article. If you need to look for the answer in the reading, the number in parentheses is a paragraph number.

1. What are two reasons that people choose products? (1)

   _____ _____

2. What are some examples of modern technology? (4)

   _____

3. Why are some consumers vulnerable?　(4, 8)

   _____

4. What are some ways consumers use the computer? (4, 5, 6, 7, 8)

_____

5. Find four words that mean a person who buys something. (1, 2, 4, 6)

_____ _____ _____

_____

Opinions

Here are some ideas from the reading and some ideas about the topic. Read each one and check *I agree, I disagree,* or *I'm not sure.*

1. Advertising can create a desire for a product.
   ❏ I agree.   ❏ I disagree.   ❏ I'm not sure.

2. Advertising helps businesses to compete for customers.
   ❏ I agree.   ❏ I disagree.   ❏ I'm not sure.

3. Using computers to shop is a good idea.
   ❏ I agree.   ❏ I disagree.   ❏ I'm not sure.

4. Convenience is important to shoppers.
   ❏ I agree.   ❏ I disagree.   ❏ I'm not sure.

5. Consumers should be cautious with their credit card numbers.
   ❏ I agree.   ❏ I disagree.   ❏ I'm not sure.

Main Ideas

Each of the three headings below states a main idea. Copy these headings onto a separate sheet of paper to make your own chart. The list of phrases and sentences gives details about the three main ideas. Read each phrase and sentence, choose some key words from that item, and decide which main idea it supports. Write the key words of each phrase or sentence under the heading. Then discuss your answers with your classmates.

> The Reasons Manufacturers Advertise
> Computer Shopping
> The Vulnerable Consumer

People pay bills on-line.
Advertisements influence customers.
Advertising influences a customer's choices.
Some sellers are dishonest.
comparison-shopping
making reservations at home
You can find the products that are difficult to find in stores.
Some shoppers charge too much on their credit cards.
keeping track of finances
beautiful clothes on a beautiful woman on the television shopping channel
Advertising is good business.
Some products are not as good as their ads.
Colorful, moving advertisements are effective.
The shopping channel demonstrates appliances.
The windows of the stores have interesting models of clothes and shoes.
The cost of returning merchandise is expensive.

Inferences

In this article, the writer describes shopping as convenient, time-saving, money-saving, and entertaining. The opposites are inconvenient, time-wasting, high cost, and involving work. For each of these situations, choose words that describe the shopping experience. Then discuss your inferences with a classmate.

1. A shopper sits at her computer and selects clothing for her children.

   convenient   inconvenient   time-saving   time-wasting

   money-saving   high cost   entertaining   involving work

2. A customer goes to the mall and visits five men's stores to find a particular kind of shirt at the best price.

convenient	money-saving	time-saving	entertaining
inconvenient	high cost	time-wasting	involving work

3. A home shopper looks through five catalogs and makes a list of ten items. She calls the catalog companies and uses her credit card to order the items.

convenient	money-saving	time-saving	entertaining
inconvenient	high cost	time-wasting	involving work

4. A person who is looking for a new car goes to the Internet. She searches for a used car and finds one. It is available in a city 500 miles away, but at a good price.

convenient	money-saving	time-saving	entertaining
inconvenient	high cost	time-wasting	involving work

5. A man turns on the shopping channel on television to try to find gifts for all the members of his family. He watches for four hours, finds ideal gifts, and orders them.

convenient	money-saving	time-saving	entertaining
inconvenient	high cost	time-wasting	involving work

Vocabulary Building

Practice with these words and learn more about them. Key words are in **bold** type. The paragraph numbers will help you.

1. Matt Chung decided to buy a computer for his work at the university. So he did some **comparison-shopping**. He feels that he spent his money well. (1)

   What did Matt do?

   a. He bought a good computer for a high price.

   b. He saw a lot of computers in a lot of stores.

   c. He compared the best points of many computers before buying.

2. Two important **agricultural** products from Canada are wheat and potatoes. Huge farms produce much more than Canada can use.

   Where do agricultural products come from?

   a. wheat   b. manufacturers   c. farms

3. Advertising displays inform shoppers about products for sale in the store. Each store advertises its products in an attractive way. Shoppers analyze the products by looking at the displays.

   The **advertising** helps the business…

   a. analyze.   b. compete.   c. produce.

4. The shopper saw some **discount coupons** in the newspaper. She took them with her when she went shopping at the mall.

   She probably…

   a. mailed the coupons to the manufacturer.

   b. got a bargain at the mall.

   c. parked in a large parking lot.

5. Many customers shop from their homes. They use catalogs, computers, and televisions.

   Why are they **vulnerable**?

   a. Modern technology is dangerous, and people can get hurt.

   b. They can pay in several payments, or installments.

   c. Spending a lot of money is too easy with technology.

6. What do careful shoppers do before they buy? Most people look at the advertising displays. They consider the prices of several dealers. They **analyze** their choices. Then they make their decisions.

   These buyers are…

   a. vulnerable   b. rational   c. dishonest

Vocabulary Journal

Choose five words from the Vocabulary in Context list to be your target words. Write the words here:

_____ _____ _____ _____ _____

Now write them in your vocabulary journal. Remember to include the following parts:
- your target word
- the sentence from the Main Reading in which your target word appears
- a definition, including the part of speech
- some sentences of your own

Related Reading

Electric Cars

1   Here are some facts about cars in North America:
- Almost every family has a car.
- Some families have more than one car.
- There are at least 190 million vehicles in the United States alone.
- Every year American vehicles travel 2.2 trillion miles, or 12,000 round trips to the sun.
- Nearly ninety-eight percent (98%) of these vehicles use gasoline for fuel.
- The use of so much gasoline is a serious matter. It causes a world problem.

2   Gasoline comes from oil; oil is the raw material from the Earth that is used for many important products. However, the world's supply of oil, petroleum, is running out. In other words, petroleum is a non-renewable resource. When the supply of this important raw material is gone, there will be no more. Furthermore, oil is important for all the people on Earth—not just those with cars.

We make many important products like medicines and plastic materials from oil—it is wrong, in the opinions of many people, to burn oil up in cars.

3   Another problem with using gasoline in cars is pollution. Gasoline produces energy to make cars move, but it also produces dangerous gases, air pollution. California, for example, is a place with large numbers of cars and large, complex road systems. California also has a lot of fog—thick clouds near the surface of the Earth. This fog mixes with dirty air and becomes smog. In other words, one of the results of burning gasoline in automobiles is "smoke," a polluting emission. This dirty air is part of harmful smog. [fog + smoke or emissions = smog.] People breathe it, and many get sick from it. Carbon dioxide (CO_2) is another product from the burning of gasoline. CO_2 is harmful because it pollutes our environment and makes smog more dangerous.

4   In some areas, people are making laws to help clean the environment. California needs such laws and has them. According to one law, the vehicles in California must not emit dangerous by-products: they must have zero emissions. The California law is interesting because it made change necessary. The law gave automobile manufacturers until 1998 to make 2% of all vehicles zero-emission vehicles (ZEVs). The lawmakers gave manufacturers until 2003 to make 10%, or about 22,000, of all vehicles ZEVs. One kind of ZEV is the electric car. Electric cars emit no smog-producing pollutants like gasoline vehicles do. They do not burn anything. But automobile makers and car dealers say, "People will not buy electric cars." They give two reasons. According to the makers and the sellers, ZEVs will cost more than ordinary cars. Also, they need to stop frequently for more energy. People will not be able to take long trips in ZEVs because the cars will have to stop often for power. This process will take more time than it takes to fill a gas tank with gasoline.

5   The manufacturers have another solution to the problems. They want to change the gasoline by making it cleaner. They say that they can produce gasoline that makes fewer dangerous emissions. However, that is probably not the answer because there will be more and more cars in the future. Thus the increased number of cars will produce more and more pollution—even if each car makes less. Another solution is that vehicles should be able to use other fuels. Some fuel does not cause as much pollution as gasoline. In 2000, the state of Arizona paid part of the cost for people who bought alternative fuel vehicles.

6   Some manufacturers are already producing electric cars. American, Japanese, and French automakers are producing electric cars. They planned to produce more than 200,000 electric cars in 2000 and more each following year. It is likely that many other places will pass laws like the California law. So in the future, cars will use renewable energy—electricity. More important, if the electricity is made by wind or water, the cars will not pollute our planet. Electric cars make good anti-pollution sense. And soon they may be economical, dependable, and convenient.

General Comprehension

Circle the letter of the item that best completes each sentence.

1. Almost every family in North America…
   a. drives an electric car.   c. wants to drive a ZEV.
   b. has at least one car.   d. has 190 million cars.

2. Every year American vehicles travel…
   a. 190 million miles.   c. 190 trillion miles.
   b. 2.2 trillion miles.   d. 2.2 million miles.

3. Gasoline emissions…
   a. are smoke and CO_2.
   b. are running out.
   c. are good for the environment.
   d. are laws in California.

4. Just California…
   a. has 190 million cars.
   b. has a ZEV law.
   c. produces ZEVs.
   d. emits smog.

5. California's law says that…
   a. cars must travel 2.2 trillion miles.
   b. cars must travel every day.
   c. 10% of the cars there must be ZEV by 2003.
   d. 2% of all cars must be ZEV now.

Vocabulary Building

1. **Smog** is an example of pollution in our environment.
   Smog is…
   a. carbon dioxide and oxygen.
   b. dirty air and fog.
   c. gasoline and oil.
   d. smoke and dirty air.

2. Oil is a **non-renewable** material.
   Non-renewable means that…
   a. something is new.
   b. we can use something—if it is new.
   c. we can use something again and again.
   d. when something is used up, it is gone.

3. Gasoline vehicles produce dangerous **emissions**.
   Emissions are…
   a. the same as smog.
   b. energy from gasoline.
   c. products from burning gasoline.
   d. what causes fog.

4. Gasoline-burning vehicles produce **pollutants**.
   Pollutants are…

   a. dangerous by-products such as pollution from burning.

   b. good for the environment.

   c. zero-emission vehicles.

   d. renewable resources, such as electricity from wind power.

5. The goal is **zero** oil use for automobiles.
   Zero means…

   a. oxygen.   c. fine or good.

   b. no or none.   d. less than 100.

6. One important **resource** for all the people on Earth is oil.
   A **resource** is a…

   a. law.   c. ZEV, a zero-emission vehicle.

   b. supply of raw material.   d. reason and a result.

7. The main idea of this article is that…

   a. families in North America have more than one car.

   b. electric cars are good for the environment.

   c. vehicle emissions pollute the environment.

   d. the supply of oil is running out.

Opinions

Would you want an electric car? On a separate sheet of paper, make two lists. Give each list a head: *Reasons to Buy One* and *Reasons Not to Buy One*. Discuss your reasons with a partner.

Related Reading

Why People Buy

1   Why do people buy? Why do people choose to buy certain products? These are important questions for manufacturers and businesses. One of the reasons is advertising. Manufacturers know that effective advertisements sell products. They understand people's behavior in the marketplace. They have studied the psychology of advertising and buying. Manufacturers analyze the business of selling and buying all the time. This is called market research. They know all the different motives that influence a consumer's purchase. Only some of the reasons for buying are rational; most of the reasons are emotional.

2   The business of selling in the marketplace is competitive. Manufacturers compete for special display places. In a grocery store, each one wants to own the eye-level display. Many shoppers do not purchase products from the top or bottom shelves. The customer is often in a hurry, and the customer is human. Therefore, the customer buys the product within easy reach. Shoppers buy more products that they can see easily. On television, examples of special display places include commercials, or advertisements, during major sports events, like the World Cup, the Olympics, the hockey championships, and the Super Bowl. Manufacturers pay large amounts of money to advertise their products on television because millions of people see these games. Other special display opportunities are ads in magazines. The best advertising spaces are on the inside of the front or back cover of the magazine. The Internet is another special display opportunity for advertisers. They put their advertisements on the Internet. A computer user who is looking for information about a special plant may see ads for flowers on the screen next to the information. Or a sports fan who is looking for the scores of a game may see ads for sports equipment. The traveler who is making rental car reservations may see ads for cars and rental agencies. The advertisements are clever and entertaining. They pop up and flash on the screen. Like the other kinds of advertising, they persuade people to buy.

3   Manufacturers and storeowners use their knowledge of why people buy. For example, they understand decision buying and impulse buying. They encourage impulse buying. For example, near the checkout counters at a lot of stores, there are large racks with many products on them. At a grocery store checkout counter, there may be collections of little books, magazines, candy, gum, razor blades, soft drinks, and other little things. These displays are very attractive. The customers go to the checkout counter to pay

for their purchases; shoppers have already made all the rational, well-thought-out decisions about buying. They are feeling good about their choices. They know that they have shopped well. However, at this point, shoppers are vulnerable. The customers stand there and wait to pay for their purchases. Their eyes move over the attractive displays of candy and the colorful pictures on the magazines. Then suddenly one customer buys something extra. The customer does not need or plan to buy candy or magazines— these are not rational decisions. However, for emotional reasons, the customer buys. What happened? Waiting for a few minutes in line, the customer picked up a magazine to look at it. Suddenly the customer decided to take the magazine home to finish an article. And that is exactly what the storeowner and manufacturer hope will happen: they expect the customer to buy for an emotional reason.

4   Buying the magazine at the checkout counter is an example of an emotional purchase. However, many purchases are just the opposite. They are rational, well thought out. Logical buyers usually think about economy, dependability, and convenience in their purchases. However, sometimes advertisements change their minds. For example, fifteen-year-old Jonathan chooses the expensive athletic shoes that he sees on the feet of a basketball star in a television commercial. His sister wants the T-shirt with the label that a beautiful model advertises. Jonathan feels like the sports hero with those shoes on his feet. The picture of the model remains in his sister's mind when she wears the T-shirt. A man may buy a suit of clothes because he sees a similar suit on an actor in a movie or television program. The purchaser wants to copy the athlete, model, or movie actor by using the same product. So the consumer buys the product, even though it is expensive. Their decisions to buy may be emotional and not necessarily rational.

5   Sometimes people have other reasons for buying. People buy things to get the attention of other people. Buying a particular car or large television set, for example, says that the person can afford it—and perhaps that the person is rich, attractive, and exciting. Other things that people buy are for pleasure—tickets to a sports event, a movie, or a concert. Of course, people buy most things because they need them. Everyone needs food, but advertising might determine the kind of food that a person buys. Knowing the reasons behind the buying decisions makes a person a better shopper.

Detail Questions: *True* or *False*?

Decide whether each statement is true or false according to the reading. Circle *true* or *false*. Write the number of the paragraph in the reading that shows the answer.

1. Manufacturers use market research.   true   false   _____

2. Business people use advertising to sell products.   true   false   _____

3. Shoppers usually make rational decisions about their purchases.   true   false   _____

4. Popular events are good places for ads.   true   false   _____

5. An ad on the back cover of a magazine is usually not an effective advertisement.   true   false   _____

6. Impulse buying is rational.   true   false   _____

7. Many Internet advertisements are clever and entertaining.   true   false   _____

8. Customers look at attractive displays while they are standing in check-out lines.   true   false   _____

9. Advertisements sometimes change the   true   false   _____
   plans that shoppers have made.

10. Shoppers make better decisions when   true   false   _____
    they understand the reasons for their
    decisions.

Main Ideas

Which of the following titles tells the main idea of the article?

    a. Buying New Products

    b. Making Good Shopping Decisions

    c. Comparison Shopping

    d. Doing Market Research

Opinions

Here are some ideas from the reading and some ideas about the topic. Read
each one, and check *I agree, I disagree,* or *I'm not sure.*

1. Emotional buying is bad business.
   ❑ I agree.   ❑ I disagree.   ❑ I'm not sure.

2. Advertising helps people learn.
   ❑ I agree.   ❑ I disagree.   ❑ I'm not sure.

3. Usually the most expensive products are the best.
   ❑ I agree.   ❑ I disagree.   ❑ I'm not sure.

4. Businesses should not be allowed to advertise on television and the
   Internet.
   ❑ I agree.   ❑ I disagree.   ❑ I'm not sure.

 **Beyond Reading**

Reflexive Pronouns

One special kind of pronoun is the reflexive pronoun: *myself, yourself, herself, himself, itself, oneself, ourselves, yourselves,* and *themselves.* In some sentences, the subject (the person who does the action) and an object (the person who receives the result of the action) are the same. The subject noun occurs twice in the sentence; it is the same as the object noun: *Alma prepared Alma for a job search.* We cannot use the simple pronoun *her.* If we do, the reader expects that Alma prepared another woman for a job search. The word part *self* is added to *her*—that's how the reader knows that Alma helped Alma (*herself*): *Alma prepared herself for a job search.*

Look at these examples:

> Sven wrote a letter to an employer about himself. (about Sven)
> Lucinda has confidence in herself. (in Lucinda)
> Mr. and Mrs. Vasquez never talk about themselves. (about Mr. and Mrs. Vasquez.)
> All of you are responsible for yourselves. (about all of you)

In other sentences, the subject noun and an adverbial expression may require a reflexive pronoun:

> They can't do it. We have to do it ourselves!
> This door is automatic; it closes by itself.

Here are some more sentences with a repeated person or an adverbial expression that uses a reflexive pronoun. Use the appropriate reflexive pronoun. Note that the subject can be repeated in many different places in the sentences.

1. Alison used a mirror to take a picture of _____ .

2. If you want a job to be done right, you have to do it
   _____ !

3. I was so lonely that I sat down and wrote _____ a letter.

4. We were hungry, so we made sandwiches for _____ .

5. That jar cover is so tight that my mother cannot open it
   _____ .

6. Arthur is four years old. He wants to do everything by

   _____ .

7. The Hills bought a new house for _____ , not for their children.

8. The bookshelf comes in pieces in a small box. You have to put it together _____ . It's a do-it-yourself kit!

9. Be careful with that knife! It's very sharp, and you could cut

   _____ .

10. A person cannot depend on others to clean up. One must do it

    _____ .

Discussion Ideas

Discuss the following situations with your classmates.

1. A friend of yours spends all her money too fast. She asks you for your opinion about what she can do to become a better shopper. Tell her what to do.
2. A new student comes to your class. The student wants to know about shopping. Discuss the advice you would give the student about shopping.

Writing Ideas

1. Bring to class some advertisements from magazines. Choose an advertisement with emotional appeal or one that has a lot of facts. Write a paragraph that describes the advertisement. What does the manufacturer want you to think? What does the advertiser expect the customer to buy? Why does the advertiser expect the customer to buy the product? Who are the customers that the advertiser expects to buy the product?
2. Here's a chance to use your imagination. You are an advertiser with a product to sell. What is your product? Give it a name. Write an advertisement to sell the product. Share your advertisement with your class.

⏱ Timed Reading 1

Human-Powered Machines

Everything about Eugene, Oregon, says "bicycles." There are bicycles and bicycle racks everywhere. The town has 85 miles of special lanes on the streets for bicycles. Many people ride their bicycles to work. Others ride just for pleasure or for good exercise. They know that riding bicycles keeps them fit. In the city there are twelve bike shops that sell bicycles and bicycle parts. There are also five manufacturers of bicycles in town. More than 350 people have jobs in these businesses. In fact, the bike business brings more than $4 million into Eugene every year. There are special parking areas for bicycles at concerts and athletic events. The city gives awards to businesses that encourage their employees to ride bikes.

It is not strange that Jan VanderTuin lives in Eugene. Jan, a bike racer, used to race in California. Then he traveled around Europe. There he saw many people using bicycles every day in their work. He learned that bicycles could be used for transportation almost anywhere. Today Jan has a shop where he builds bicycles. However, his bicycles, called "human-powered machines," are not ordinary. The riders of some of his bikes use their hands instead of their feet on the pedals. On other bikes designed by Jan, the rider almost lies on his back to ride.

Some bicycles are tricycles, with three wheels, not two. Other bikes have handlebars below the seat. These machines look strange, but they are comfortable to ride.

Jan even makes bicycles for people who are usually in wheelchairs. Truck-bicycles to carry loads are another of Jan's ideas. These machines are not as expensive as cars but are almost as fast.

Jan is also a teacher. He talks to students in local public schools and the university about transportation. University students come to his shop to learn about bikes. Part of his shop is called the Center for Appropriate Transport. People from around the world come to learn about bicycles. And Jan teaches them all—he wants people to know that using bicycles for transportation makes sense. They are economical, dependable, and convenient.

Time: _____

Now answer these questions as quickly as you can.

1. Eugene, Oregon,…
   a. is a university.   b. is a bicycle town.   c. is in Canada.

2. Bike lanes are…
   a. special places for races in California.
   b. special bicycles for people in wheelchairs.
   c. special parts of a street for bicycles.

3. Bicycles are important to Eugene because…
   a. 350 people have jobs because of bikes.
   b. $5 million comes from the bicycle business.
   c. there are 12 bike manufacturers in town.

4. At least ____ people in Eugene work for bicycle manufacturers.
   a. eighty-five   b. three hundred fifty   c. twelve

5. In Europe Jan saw…

   a. people riding bicycles in their work.

   b. bicycle riders using their hands, not their feet.

   c. three-wheeled human-powered vehicles.

6. Jan does not build bicycles that…

   a. look strange.

   b. have handlebars below the seat.

   c. cost as much as cars.

7. Most bicycle-riders use their ____ to power the bike.

   a. hands   b. handlebars   c. feet

8. The Center for Appropriate Transport is…

   a. in California.

   b. part of Jan's shop.

   c. part of a university.

9. Tricycles are different from bicycles in…

   a. the number of wheels.

   b. how the rider rides.

   c. where the handlebars are.

10. The main idea of the article is that…

    a. Eugene, Oregon, is a bicycle town.

    b. using bicycles for transportation is Jan's idea.

    c. Jan is a teacher.

Timed Reading 2

Ads: On the Internet, the Radio, Signs, and Television

The secret of good selling is good advertising. If a customer sees a product or hears the name many times, the product becomes familiar to the customer. He or she will probably buy it. That's why manufacturers have various ways of advertising products.

Customers see advertisements in magazines and newspapers. They often see television ads and hear them on radio. There can be advertisements on signs along the roads. People get advertisements in the mail. However, manufacturers are always looking for the best form of advertising. They know that the best ads demonstrate products. Customers want to see action. They want to see a moving car. Or they might buy breakfast cereal after they see a famous athlete eating the cereal. Manufacturers have worked hard to understand customers' behavior. Therefore, manufacturers want their advertisements on television and on the Internet. Television advertising has several problems, however. Advertising on television is very expensive. Another problem is that not every home has a television set. Not enough customers see the advertisements. Furthermore, television has many channels. So advertisers do not know the people who see the ads. They cannot send their ads only to people who might buy their products. Also, television ads are short. Customers see the product for less than a minute. Are television ads worth the cost?

In contrast, Internet advertising has many advantages over television. A television ad is 30 to 60 seconds long. On the Internet, the shopper can look at the ad longer. Customers have more time to see the product. Advertisers can give more information about the product. Another advantage is that an Internet ad costs less. Furthermore, shoppers see the Internet advertisement because they want to buy the product. Shoppers are not always looking for a product, but they see the ad anyway. Manufacturers can put their advertisements about a ski resort on the computer screens of people who have skis. For example, when people are looking for skis and they see an ad about a ski resort, they may make reservations at the resort. The ad is effective. The manufacturer made a sale.

Time: _____

Now answer these questions as quickly as you can.

1. An ad is an…

   a. addition.   b. advertisement.   c. advantage.

2. Good advertisements…

   a. are very short.

   b. may use a telephone.

   c. show the customer action.

3. There are advertisements…

   a. on the Internet, on signs, in newspapers, on the radio, and on TV.

   b. in moving cars, breakfast cereal, and ski resorts.

   c. for manufacturers, customers, and athletes.

4. Who uses a product?

   a. the customer   b. the advertiser   c. the manufacturer

5. Television advertisements are…

   a. longer than Internet advertisements.

   b. usually 30 to 60 seconds long.

   c. better than Internet advertisements.

6. An effective advertisement…

   a. sends skis to skiers.

   b. demonstrates a product.

   c. is a sign on a road.

7. A demonstration is…

   a. a sign.   b. action.   c. like a radio.

8. An Internet advertisement is usually…

   a. not as long as a TV advertisement.

   b. more expensive than a TV advertisement.

   c. more effective than a TV ad.

9. Which sentence means the same as this one: "The manufacturer made a sale."?

   a. A customer buys the product.

   b. The manufacturer calls a customer.

   c. A person sends something.

10. The main idea of the article is that…

    a. television ads are expensive.

    b. manufacturers use technology for advertising.

    c. Internet advertising is often more effective than television advertising.

GENERATIONS

 **Preparation**

Topic

Begin with a survey of this unit. What will it be about? Where do you fit into this picture?

The year 2001 signaled the beginning of a new millennium. People in general expect that many aspects of life will change at such a milestone in history. In truth, there are changes every day. During the twenty years before the beginning of the new millennium, several changes made life different:

- Computers and data collection changed people's lives, the way business was done.
- Satellites made worldwide communications possible.
  - Fax machines made information transfer over telephone lines easy.
  - Cellular telephones meant instant communication anywhere in the world.
- In many parts of the world, growing food changed from a family farming (agriculture) to big business, agribusiness.

The foundations of society were changing. In fact, the people were changing too.

Anticipation

1. How has satellite communication (for television, cellular phones, the Internet) changed how people live? How has communication changed people?

2. How did the fax machine break down political differences?

3. What does the computer network of the Internet know about you?

4. What changes in how people live happened as a result of the technological changes?

5. How are you different from people who are older and younger than you?

Vocabulary in Context

Each of the words in **bold** type is probably a new word to you. Practice with these words and learn more about them.

Some of the numbered items do not have any words in bold type. The new words are in the choices (a, b, c, or d) for those sentences.

1. A **century** is one hundred years, and a **millennium** is a thousand years. The first millennium started in the year 1 A.D. and ended in 1000 A.D. The third millennium began in 2001. Years like 1900 and 2000 are important in history as the beginning or end of a period of time. Therefore, people call them **milestones**.

   A. A **millennium** is a period of...

      a. a thousand years.

      b. a thousand days.

      c. a thousand months.

   B. An important date, a time of change, is called a...

      a. millennium.   b. milestone.   c. period.

2. The builders started with a large cement floor to build the house on. It had only this strong **foundation**, or base, and the roof and the walls. The **life expectancy** of the house is about 100 years; it was built to last for three **generations** of a family—parents, children, and grandchildren.

   A. The foundation of a house is the ____ on which it is built.

      a. wall   b. wood   c. base

   B. Parents and children belong to different...

      a. families.   b. generations.   c. plans.

   C. The **life expectancy** of a person is...

      a. how long the person will live.

      b. its age.

      c. what it is made of.

3. One of the **population trends** today is a move from **rural** to **urban**.
   Most of the world's population, its people, used to live on farms in
   the **countryside**. There they lived with lots of nature around them.
   In the city environment, however, they face many urban problems:
   crowding, crime, noise. However, there are jobs in the cities, so we
   see a slow but definite general change in where people live. Moving
   from farm to city is a trend, a **direction** for movement.

   A. **Population** refers to…

      a. all people in general.

      b. cities.

      c. the number of people born in one year.

   B. A **population trend** is ____ among people.

      a. a crime   b. a change   c. a problem

   C. **Rural** places are…

      a. in a city.   b. in a town.   c. outside of a city.

   D. **Urban** problems are the problems of…

      a. a farmer.   b. a student.   c. a city.

   E. If you live on a farm, you do not live in an urban environment.
      You live in the…

      a. city.   b. forest.   c. countryside.

   F. Up and down, in and out, left and right, north and south—we can
      move in these ways. These are all movements in different…

      a. directions.   b. prepositions.   c. sections.

4. There is a **trend** toward more comfortable clothing. In fact, young
   people **seem to be more casual about** their clothes even at weddings
   and funerals. It is **trendy** to wear clothing made of lightweight materials.
   Only the most **conservative** people wear formal black suits.

   A. If lots of people move or change in the same way, then we have a…

      a. situation.   b. decrease.   c. trend.

   B. A person who **seems to be casual about** friendships,…

      a. might not care about friends.

      b. doesn't hurt his or her friends.

      c. has a lot of friends.

C. Clothes, words, or actions that are popular are called…

    a. trendy.   b. comfortable.   c. casual.

D. A **conservative** person…

    a. is trendy.

    b. makes changes slowly.

    c. makes changes fast.

5. Sociologists (people who study human behavior in society) have noticed several things about young people today. First, they like **to hang out** in malls, at coffeehouses, and in parks. They seem to enjoy being with their friends in large open places. Second, these young people seem to expect **privileges**—special treatment like not having to follow the rules. They also have a great deal of **manual dexterity**. That is, they can work quickly with their hands on things like computers and other electronic tools. Like all young people in the past, some things are **cool** and some things are not. Fifty or sixty years ago, teenagers all wore white sailor hats and thought those hats were wonderful. Now something else is trendy: sports clothing. There is, in fact, a **boom** in sales of sports clothes. The people who watch changes in style and taste are experts in **marketing**. They know what young people want to buy.

A. To **hang out** in a place is to…

    a. put clothes in something.

    b. spend time there.

    c. buy things.

B. Which of these items is a **privilege**?

    a. having permission to park a car where no one else can park

    b. drinking coffee at a coffeehouse with a group of friends

    c. wearing clothes that are comfortable

C. If you have **manual dexterity**, you are most likely to be able to…

    a. make things work with your hands.

    b. know where to go to buy things.

    c. choose clothing that is trendy.

D. If a person or some clothing is **cool**, then that clothing or that person is…

    a. saying something about the weather.

    b. very positive, popular, or trendy.

    c. probably of little value or worth.

E. A great **increase** in business or sales is a…

    a. style.

    b. taste.

    c. boom.

F. People who are interested in **marketing** are most likely to work in…

    a. the business of selling.

    b. the coffeehouse business.

    c. the computer business.

Main Reading

Generations

1   Who you are, what you want, and how you act are related to generation values. According to marketing expert Cynthia R. Cohen of Strategic MindShare, Inc. (strategicmindshare.com), the year of your birth tells a lot about you. For example, to Cohen, people born between 1988 and 1998 are "Speeders." These people need to have more than one focus of interest at every moment.

2   According to two sociologists, Neil Howe and William Strauss, people who were born in 1982 or after 1982 are "the Millennials." It is their generation name. Howe, Strauss, and Cohen all agree: these people are different from older people. We can expect certain kinds of behaviors from them.

3   Both Cohen and the Howe-Strauss team have names for other generations, too. Cohen's model looks like this:

Birth Years	Generation Name
before 1943	the Grays
1944-1965	Boomers
1966-1976	Generation X
1977-1987	Generation Y
1988-1998	Speeders

4   The Howe-Strauss Model looks like this:

Birth Years	Generation Name
before 1900	the Lost Generation
1901-1924	the World War II Generation (also known as the Swing Generation and G.I. Generation)
1925-1942	the Silent Generation
1943-1960	(Baby) Boomers
1961-1981	Generation X
1982-	the Millennials

5   Cohen's model reflects how people buy. Howe and Strauss's model reflects other aspects of personality. Names for generations before 1960 are really North American labels. However, since 1960, the world has become more and more connected. The global village idea fits most urban people of the world today. A teenager in a modern Asian city has much in common with teenagers in South American cities and European cities. Communication is making the world seem smaller. As communication increases, people around the world will share more ideas and values.

      Let's look first at Cohen's model:

6   The Grays, who were born before 1943, were the first rock 'n' roll generation. They love Elvis Presley and know why he was so great (because he was so different in his music). The name *Buddy Holly* (a man who made rock 'n' roll music very popular) means something to them. The Grays are the generation that saw

the beginning of shopping malls. They tend to have large net worth (a lot of money in things that they own) but not much expendable cash (little money to spend). That is, they own property like homes and cars, but they don't have a lot of money in the bank to spend. As teenagers, they did not have cars, but they had jobs.

7   The Baby Boomers, or just Boomers, were born between 1944 and 1965. They made the Beatles famous. This generation values material things like nice cars and pretty houses. They wanted to have lots of money. They also value youth, so they have plastic surgery and buy anything to seem younger. They enjoy spending money. They live in large houses, and many of them spend more than they have. The Boomers are the grandparents of most of the children in school today.

8   Cohen's Generation X was born between 1966 and 1976. These young people in their twenties and thirties are the most powerful part of society. They are the ones buying expensive items like houses. They are comfortable with e-commerce. They are responsible for relaxed dress codes—they prefer comfortable clothes to formal business clothes, so they changed the style. This generation wants good quality and good design. They like to go out in the evening; they go to popular restaurants and lounges for food and entertainment. They set the styles, and they make certain places successful. Gen Xers have power in business. These young adults might smoke cigarettes even though they know it is bad for them. They tend to be more casual about drugs and sex than Boomers.

9   Cohen says that between 1977 and 1987 comes another generation. She calls it Generation Y. Many of these young people are college age. They are excellent consumers. People of Gen Y are stuck in the middle, not sure where they are going. However, Generation Y is the reason for a lot of research in marketing. They shop by reputation, preferring well-known brand names.

They were the first to make it trendy (popular) to go out to get coffee. They started the boom in coffeehouses while they were in high school. Generation Y people have a few symbols that distinguish them from Generation X. For example, they hang out a lot, just sitting and relaxing with friends. They are "mall rats." They like open areas like malls and coffeehouse as their social setting. They are more conservative about drugs and sex than Gen X. Also, unlike Generation X, Generation Y students expect privileges. They want people to help them.

10   Between 1988 and 1998, according to Cohen, the Speeders were born. The name is appropriate because these young people seem fast in every aspect of their lives. They know the Internet and can find information on-line in five minutes. They are influencers, and they influence what the Grays are buying (grandparents for grandchildren). They understand technology without much work. Ten-year-olds with PDAs can figure them out fast. Speeders are tech-savvy (knowledgeable about technology). They have light-speed manual and mental dexterity (hand and brain work together fast). They are brand-makers and -breakers. If a particular store is "cool" to them, they buy there. Speeders are the reason that the store is doing so well right now. Furthermore, many Speeders have multilingual abilities, and they like multitasking (doing several things at once). Their thinking skills (cognitive abilities) are connected with technology. Technology is part of life. Cohen says, "Take a 12-year-old with you to buy a computer. The 12-year-old will KNOW."

11   Howe and Strauss (www.millennialsrising.com) have similar ideas about the generations. They believe that the Millennials will be a "hero" generation. These two sociologists point out an important fact of history. The values and norms of society seem to follow a pattern. Every four generations, a hero generation occurs. The last hero generation was the World War II generation.

The people of this generation performed great deeds. They built dams, cities, and great road systems. They fought wars, conquered diseases, and went to the moon. Now, four generations later, sociologists are predicting the same kind of generation, a generation of achievers. We can, these experts say, expect great things from the Millennials.

12   Howe and Strauss look back into history to make this prediction. The life expectancy since the middle 1500s has increased from fifty years to about eighty years. Even so, about every fifty to sixty years, there is a hero generation. Therefore, within almost every person's lifetime, there is one generation of heroes. There are also self-centered generations (like the Baby Boomers). They paid other people (babysitters) to take care of their children. They went to play golf. Then there are generations that didn't seem to follow the rules (like the Lost Generation and Generation X). There is also the Silent Generation. These senior citizens today were children during a world war. They value peace and diplomacy. They are not strong leaders. For example, there is no American president from the Silent Generation. The Silent Generation are not heroes. The world is ready for a hero generation. And the Speeders or Millennials (whatever you decide to call them) may be the next generation of great people.

Detail Questions: *True* or *False*?

Decide whether each statement is *true* or *false* according to the reading. Also write the number of the paragraph with the answer.

1. Cynthia R. Cohen is a sociologist.   true   false   _____

2. *Speeders* and *Millennials* refer to the same   true   false   _____
   group of people.

3. A hero generation comes every   true   false   _____
   one hundred years.

4. Today's senior citizens lived through   true   false   _____
   a world war.

5. The oldest generation alive today, according   true   false   _____
   to Howe and Strauss, is Generation Y.

6. The person who can help a senior citizen   true   false   _____
   buy a computer is probably twelve years old.

7. We call the people of a generation by a name.   true   false   _____

8. The Grays have lots of cash in their pockets   true   false   _____
   to spend.

9. Older people know more about technology   true   false   _____
   than young people.

10. Generation X doesn't have much influence   true   false   _____
    on business anymore.

General Comprehension

Try to answer the questions without looking at the article.

1. Which generation has light-speed manual dexterity? _____

2. In the United States, which generation did not produce a president?

   _____

3. Which generation likes to walk around the mall or sit in a park?

   _____

4. Which generation hired babysitters to take care of their children?

   _____

5. Which generations are grandparents now? _____

6. What great things did the last hero generation do? _____

7. Who were the people of the last hero generation? _____

8. Which generation went to the moon? _____

9. What do malls, parks, and coffeehouses have in common that young people like? _____

10. Which generations don't seem to follow the rules of society?

_____

Opinions

1. "A hero generation is a group of people who are achievers." What does this sentence mean for the youngest generation now?

2. Which name do you like better, Speeders or Millennials? Why?

3. According to Cohen, which generation are you part of? Do you feel as if you fit the description?

4. According to Howe and Strauss, which is your generation? Do you feel that you fit in their definition?

Main Ideas

A. This main reading is about two different ideas about generations. One view is the view of business/marketing. The other is a sociological view (how people fit into a community/sociology).

Read the terms and names. Which view does each belong to, *business* or *community*? Write the terms and names under the headings. Note that some of the phrases belong to both groups. Write them under both headings.

Boomers	Millennials	Cynthia R. Cohen
Speeders	Generation Y	The Lost Generation
the Grays	Generation X	The Silent Generation
Neil Howe	William Strauss	

Business

_____

_____

_____

_____

_____

_____

Community

_____

_____

_____

_____

_____

_____

B. Choose a good title for this main reading. (Put a check [✓] in front of each of the titles that is appropriate.)

_____   Cohen, Howe, and Strauss

_____   Differences in Generations

_____   When Were You Born?

_____   The Wonderful Boomer Generation

_____   Two Generation Models

Inferences

1. In the following sentence, what is a PDA? "Ten-year-olds with PDAs can figure them out fast. Speeders are tech-savvy (knowledgeable about technology)."

   a. a television program

   b. something electronic

   c. a kind of book

2. How old is a senior citizen?

   a. between 25 and 35

   b. over 40 years old

   c. over 60 years of age

3. People _____ something that is "cool."

   a. like   b. don't like   c. never buy

4. The Silent Generation probably got that name because…

   a. they were quiet people and did not have opinions.

   b. they didn't show much leadership ability.

   c. they grew up during a world war.

5. The global village probably refers to the fact that…

   a. there are a lot of cities in many places around the world now.

   b. people live in the same typical villages everywhere.

   c. people all over the world need one another, like people in a small community.

6. What does *life expectancy* mean in the following sentence? "The life expectancy since the middle 1500s has increased from fifty years to about eighty years."

    a. how long people live

    b. what people think they will get out of life

    c. what happened to people in the 1500s

7. Around the world the people born ____ are most alike because of the increase in world communication.

    a. after 1988   c. before 1987

    b. between 1944 and 1965   d. after 1943

8. What does this sentence probably mean? "(Speeders) are brand-makers and -breakers."

    a. If Speeders like something, they break it.

    b. If Speeders like something, they buy a lot of it and it becomes trendy.

    c. Speeders make new brands of things, and they break things then.

9. What does this sentence probably mean? "Their thinking skills (cognitive abilities) are connected with technology."

    a. They act like computers.

    b. They understand computers naturally.

    c. They need computers to live.

10. People who live through a war are most likely to value...

    a. technology.   b. peace.   c. new ideas.

Vocabulary Building

The words in **bold** type are probably new words for you.

1. Members of Generation X are comfortable with **e-commerce**.
   What do they find natural and easy to do?

2. Members of Generation X are responsible for **relaxed dress codes**.
   What do they like to wear?

3. The last **hero generation** was the World War II generation.
   What did the people of this generation do?

4. The doctors of that time **conquered** diseases.

   What happened to the diseases?

5. The people of this generation are **college age**.

   They are between _____ and _____ years of age.

6. The Grays tend to have a **large net worth** but not much **expendable** cash.

   Which sentence below is true about the Grays?

   a. They own houses and cars, but they don't have money in their pockets.

   b. They have a lot of money, but they don't want to spend it.

   c. They have earned a lot of money, but they don't have any left.

7. People of Gen Y are **stuck in the middle**.

   a. People of Generation Y do not have opinions.

   b. The people of Generation Y are neither old nor young.

   c. Generation Y people are between two other powerful generations.

8. A person who is **"savvy"** about a topic…

   a. is learning about the topic.

   b. thinks about the topic a lot because he or she wants to learn about it.

   c. understands the topic.

Vocabulary Journal

Choose five words from the Vocabulary in Context list to be your target words. Write the words here:

_____ _____ _____ _____ _____

Now write them in your vocabulary journal. Remember to include the following parts:

- your target word
- the sentence from the Main Reading in which your target word appears
- a definition, including the part of speech
- some sentences of your own

Related Reading

Making a Bridge Over the Generation Gap

1 A generation gap is just a difference in values and beliefs between parents and children. Sociologists began to use this term in the 1960s. "Generation gap" is a useful concept because people in different age groups have different experiences. Communication can become difficult between parents and children. Some parents feel that their children's peers (friends the same age) have more influence over them than their families. These parents fear that they will "lose" their children. This feeling of differences between parents and offspring is the generation gap.

2 Do we have generation gaps in today's society? The consensus, the opinion of experts, is that the generation gap may not be a serious problem anymore. Sociologists believe that in some matters, like music and fashion, there are differences. Young people tend to agree with their contemporaries. However, on issues such as belief in right and wrong, young people tend to believe the same things as their parents. They ask Mom and Dad for help with important questions like career goals.

3 Counselors have some important suggestions for parents to use with their teenage or young-adult children. These ideas seem to improve communication.

- Suggestion 1: A parent should be a good listener. Young people need to express their feelings and opinions. A mother and father who listen can help a young person speak openly. Openness usually means honesty between the two generations. A parent tries to help a young adult learn to be independent not by questioning but by listening.

- Suggestion 2: A parent should be respectful to a child. A parent should show trust toward the child. A young adult believes in his or her parents' judgment. If Dad treats him like an adult, a young man is more likely to act like an adult. If Mom shows that she believes in her daughter, the young woman will act responsibly.

- Suggestion 3: In talking with a young person, a parent should stay calm. It's not easy for a parent to watch his or her child make mistakes. Therefore, the parent should talk to the young person in terms of thinking about the results. Getting angry doesn't help anyone. In general, for good communication, a person should avoid starting a sentence with "you."

- Suggestion 4: A parent should avoid "lectures." That is, a parent should ask a teenager if he or she wants an opinion. If the answer is no, the parent says nothing more. If the young person wants an opinion, the parent should not expect agreement. The parent should say, "This is my view."

- Suggestion 5: Use "I" messages instead of "you" messages. This idea is important for all communication, not just between generations. "I" know how "I" feel. I do not know how you feel. Therefore, I should say, "I don't understand." And not "You are not speaking clearly."

- Suggestion 6: Both parents and children must live according to the same rules. Parents are models, or examples, for their children. Children lose respect for parents who do not follow the rules. A child sees a parent behaving in a responsible way, and the child learns to act the same way. Actions speak louder than words.

4   Furthermore, parents should let their teenagers and young adults know about their feelings. A parent should apologize if he or she makes a mistake. A young person needs to know that parents are human beings.

5   The teenage years are seldom easy for either child or parent. The young person is learning to become an adult. And the parent is learning to give the child freedom to become an adult. These suggestions of ways to interact can help to improve communication between the generations. The parents feel closer to their children and can support them. The teenagers and young adults feel the loving support from their parents.

Main Ideas

1. The main idea of paragraph 1:
   a. A difference in values and beliefs between any two people is a generation gap.
   b. The generation gap is a place in society.
   c. Difficult communication between parents and teenage children is the generation gap.
   d. Parents are afraid that they will lose their children.

2. The main idea of paragraph 2:

   a. Young people like loud music.

   b. Today the differences between parents and children are not as serious as they were a few years ago.

   c. The differences in values between parents and children is not important.

   d. Teenagers want their parents to help them with their career goals.

3. The main idea of paragraph 3:

   a. Suggestions for parents to be good listeners and to respect their young adult children can improve communication.

   b. A parent should always talk to a teenager about the teenager's opinions.

   c. The most important thing in a family is to make rules that everyone follows.

   d. A parent must be a good model of behavior for a child.

4. The main idea of paragraph 4:

   a. Parents do not have feelings.

   b. Teenagers cannot understand their parents.

   c. Parents should share their feelings with their children.

   d. Parents should apologize if they make mistakes.

5. The main idea of paragraph 5:

   a. The teenage years are not easy for parent or child.

   b. It is important to communicate with one's children.

   c. Generations can probably not communicate well.

   d. A teenager is learning to be an adult.

Vocabulary Building

Look at the words and phrases in the list. Find pairs of words or phrases that match in meaning. They should fit together into the sentences below.

~~trust~~	beliefs	feelings	examples
peers	models	children	age group
issues	~~respect~~	opinions	generation
values	express	behavior	speak openly
actions	matters	offspring	contemporaries

1. If a parent or teacher gives both _____*trust*_____ and

   _____*respect*_____ to a young person, that person will act in a

   responsible way.

2. A person's _____ and _____ are other

   people about the same age.

3. In some places a person can say what he or she wants to say; he or

   she can _____ and _____ about his or

   her ideas.

4. Children generally keep the _____ and _____

   of their parents, although they may like different music and different

   styles of clothing.

5. The people of every _____ or _____ seem

   to have different ideas about fashion and style.

6. Parents and children might disagree on _____ like

   music and style, but they agree on the big _____ .

7. The older people in a society are _____ or

   _____ for younger people; the younger people learn

   how to behave from the older folks.

8. A person will not understand you if you don't tell him or her your

    _____ and your _____ about topics like

    life goals.

9. Parents' sons and daughters are their _____ , their

    _____ .

10. _____ speak louder than words; you can know a person

    from his or her _____ .

Discussion Ideas

Discuss the following situations with your classmates.

1. There are some parts of "growing up" that are not easy for young
   people. Make a list of some of life's challenges (which young people
   have). Choose one to talk about with a partner, and report to your
   classmates.
2. Is it right to put people into generation groups? Do all people of an
   age group really act alike? What are your opinions?

Writing Ideas

1. A *stereotype* is a general statement about a group of people or a set
   of things or events. For example, "People from Sweden are blond and
   blue-eyed." It is true that many Swedish people have blue eyes and
   blond hair, but not all do. Stereotypes about groups of people are
   usually unfair statements. These generalizations can hurt people's
   feelings because they are judgments about people. The two readings
   about generations contain several stereotypes. Look at them to find a
   statement that you think is a stereotype. Write a paragraph to show
   why this statement is not true.
2. State a stereotype about one age group and show what is true about it.

Timed Reading 1

A Name for the Baby

Is there anything as trendy as names? Sociologists sometimes study which names are common and why. From generation to generation, some names lose their place quickly. New names take their place. Other names are old standards. These names remain popular for centuries. The name *John* is one such name. John is the strongest of names. For centuries nearly every family has at least one John. For women, the names *Susan* and *Elizabeth* have the same kind of popularity. These names never seem to go out of style.

In every generation, some names become popular quickly. Sometimes the name belongs first to a famous person, like a singer or a movie star. Unusual names like *Demi* for a girl or *Conan* for a boy obviously come from heroes on the big screen. Other times the names simply multiply. There are hundreds of thousands of *Jennifers* and *Joshuas* who are adults today. No one knows why. Each mother thought she was picking a nice name, and not one that was so popular that it was almost too common!

Parents sometimes worry their child might have the wrong name. Studies prove that a person's name can affect others' opinions of him or her. A person with a "loser" name, a name that is out of fashion, has a hard time in school. Other children make fun of the name, so the child tends to be unhappy at school. Furthermore, teachers actually expect less of the child with an unusual name. They give less attention to the child, and they don't talk as much to the child. A name can be a dangerous thing!

There are some interesting trends in new names. Many babies are being named surnames (last names). Furthermore, such names are usually unisex (the same for boys and girls). Examples include Bailey, Campbell, Chandler, Chase, Tanner, Cole, Murphy, Hayden, and Emerson.

Some of the old names are coming back. Therefore, boys' names such as *Zachary, Matthew,* and *Jacob* are common again. *Michael* has been popular for years.

Girls' names like Hannah, Mary, Ann, Samantha, Sarah, and Emily have been around for many years.

Time: _____

Now answer these questions as quickly as you can.

1. A person's surname is the same as...
   a. his or her family name.
   b. his or her first name.
   c. his father's first name.

2. The name ____ is the strongest man's name.
   a. Jacob   b. Michael   c. John

3. The name ____ can be either a boy's name or a girl's name.
   a. Henry   b. Hayden   c. Sarah

4. A name like *Demi* became popular because of…
   a. a movie star.
   b. an important family name.
   c. its age.

5. A wrong name for a child can mean…
   a. difficulty at school.
   b. having fun with it.
   c. going out of style.

6. Unisex names are…
   a. like last names.
   b. very short.
   c. the same for boys and girls.

7. Which of the girls' names does not go out of fashion?
   a. Emily   b. Campbell   c. Demi

8. Teachers talk less to a child with…
   a. a loser name.
   b. a surname for a first name.
   c. a common name like John.

9. Which of these names is a surname?
   a. Campbell   b. Zachary   c. Emily

10. Which of these titles would work for this article?
    a. Sarah and Her Friends
    b. A New Baby in Town
    c. Popularity in Names for Babies

Timed Reading 2

Changing Cultures

Today many people live longer lives with more physical and mental strength. The "life cycle" from childhood to adulthood and into older age is different from previous generations. How are ideas about the life cycle changing?

One American writer, Gail Sheehy, has identified some new trends in the life cycle. She separates life into decades, 10-year sections. Her definitions are optimistic and positive, and they may help people understand themselves as they grow older.

The ages between twenty and thirty are times of experimentation. People in their twenties try many new things with a lot of energy. They search for a path for their lives. Their responsibilities are not usually serious, and they can experiment with lifestyles choices. But when they become thirty, they pass to a stage called "First Adulthood." In this stage of life, people begin to think for themselves. They become independent and more ambitious. They begin to define themselves within society.

In the next stage of life, the forties, people begin to prepare themselves for leadership positions. Gail Sheehy sees people in their forties as working hard. They want to be successful. They have to take care of their families and begin to be masters of their work and themselves. She calls moving from this stage into the fifties the passage to the "Age of Mastery." People in their fifties have new positive feelings. They begin to see different things they can do with their lives. They become adventurers. They also begin to question their values. They want to live their lives better, with more truth. They struggle to understand the world and themselves.

She calls the next stage the "Age of Integrity." When people become sixty, they want to live their lives with real values. They work to keep their minds active. They recommit themselves to their families with love. They begin to take some active risk-taking for the future. It is a time of real maturity. Ms. Sheehy calls people in their seventies wise, people in their eighties free, and those in their nineties noble. The life cycle Ms. Sheehy writes about is long and hopeful.

Time: _____

Now answer these questions as quickly as you can.

According to the article

1. The "life cycle" is…
   a. a part of life.
   b. from childhood to adulthood to old age.
   c. people living longer.

2. Gail Sheehy is…
   a. an American writer.
   b. a part of the "Age of Mastery"
   c. a risk-taker.

3. A decade is…
   a. five years.   b. ten years.   c. twenty years.

4. People in their twenties…
   a. are mature.   b. are powerful.   c. try new things.

5. People in their thirties…
   a. are independent.   b. are leaders.   c. try new things.

6. People in their forties…
   a. are masters of their work.
   b. are more independent.
   c. have new positive feelings.

7. People in their sixties…
   a. are free.
   b. are masters of their work.
   c. want to have real values.

8. The "Age of Integrity" describes people in their…
   a. forties.   b. fifties.   c. sixties.

9. What does Ms. Sheehy call people in their seventies?
   a. free.   b. smart.   c. wise.

10. What is the best title for this reading?
    a. How to Master Life
    b. New Life Cycles Across Time
    c. Youthful Hopes

THE
CHANGING
CLIMATE

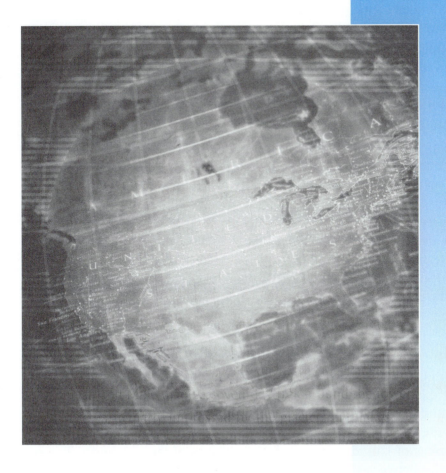

📖 Preparation

Survey this unit. Note the pictures, graphs, and illustrations. What ideas do you expect to be discussed?

Topic

Weather is the day-to-day condition of our world, where we are. **Weather** is an everyday topic of conversation. It includes the temperature, the air pressure, the wind, and the amount of rain or snow. **Climate** is general weather in a large area or region: hot and dry, cold and wet, warm and mild, hot and wet, or humid. **Weather** is part of climate.

- How is the weather today?
- What is the climate like where you are living?
- What is the climate like where you come from?
- Is this chapter probably more about **weather** or **climate**? Why?

Anticipation

1. Look at the drawing of the globe. You may remember how to find places on a globe from a geography class in school. The lines from the North Pole to the South Pole are the **longitudinal** lines. Geographers use them to measure distances from east to west from the prime meridian. We measure these distances in degrees. A degree is 1/360th of a circle. Each degree is divided into 60 smaller sections. The word *minute* (pronounced mi-NOOT) means "small." So the word *minute* is a minute part of a degree. A minute is also divided into 60 smaller parts, a second level of "minute-ness" (60 seconds). In a similar way, an hour is sixty minutes long. Each minute is divided into 60 seconds. (That's where the words *minute* and *second* came from!) The prime meridian is 0° (zero degrees) longitude. There are 360 degrees around a globe.

2. There are also lines *around* the globe. These lines go from east to west. These are lines of **latitude**. They measure distance north or south from the **equator**. We measure latitude in degrees, too. The equator is at 0° latitude. **Latitudinal** lines define geographical regions around the world. For example, the **tropics** are generally those areas between 23½ degrees of latitude south and 23½ degrees of latitude north. The sun moves between these two tropics as the seasons change. Therefore, the tropical region includes the equator.

Fill in the blanks above the illustration of the globe using these underlined items:

<u>The Tropic of Cancer:</u>	the region between the equator and latitude 23½ degrees north
<u>The Tropic of Capricorn:</u>	the region between the equator and latitude 23½ degrees south
<u>The Antarctic Circle:</u>	the region from the South Pole to latitude 66 degrees, 33 minutes south
<u>The Arctic Circle:</u>	the region from the North Pole to latitude 66 degrees, 33 minutes north
<u>High latitudes north:</u>	the region between latitudes 60 degrees north and 45 degrees north
<u>High latitudes south:</u>	the region between latitudes 60 degrees south and 45 degrees south
<u>Mid latitudes south:</u>	the region between latitudes 45 degrees south and 30 degrees south
<u>Mid latitudes north:</u>	the region between latitudes 45 degrees north and 30 degrees north

1. _____   5. _____

2. _____   6. _____

3. _____   7. _____

4. _____   8. _____

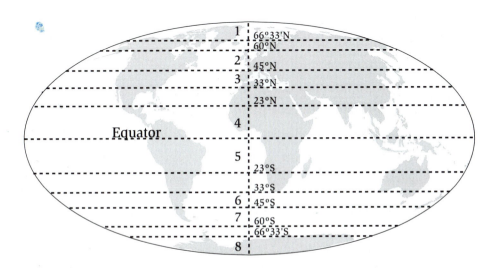

3. The word part *sub* means "below" or "less than." Where do you think the subtropics are? Give the latitudes for both northern and southern subtropical regions.

North: _____ _____

South: _____ _____

Where are the subarctic regions? Write the latitudes for both north and south subarctic regions.

North: _____ _____

South: _____ _____

4. To talk about the climate of the world, we often use terms to describe similar regions in both the Northern and Southern Hemispheres. We call warm areas "the tropics." The north and south are the "arctic zones." Think about the countries that you are familiar with. Are they in different climate regions? Is their climate similar to other countries' in the same region, either in the Northern or Southern Hemisphere? Discuss the similarities and differences in climate with your classmates.

What are some of the things that might influence, or affect, world climate? Write a check (✔) in front of each item that you think might influence climate.

_____ changes in ocean temperatures

_____ polluted river water

_____ increased use of automobiles

_____ cutting wood for fuel

_____ clearing forests for agriculture

_____ the sun's rays

_____ smoke from industry

_____ changes in the atmosphere

_____ volcano eruptions

_____ earthquakes

_____ windstorms

_____ thunderstorms

_____ snow

Vocabulary in Context

Each of the words in **bold** type is probably a new word to you. Practice with these words and learn more about them.

1. There was a small village far from other populated areas. It did not have electricity until this year. The government built solar collectors to use the sun's energy to bring **essential** refrigeration for food storage and lights to this **rural** village. This energy was necessary for the people's good health. Along with the solar collectors, several large windmills have been built to **generate** electricity. Making electrical power from wind is clean and effective.

   A. **Essential** means _____ .

   B. **Rural** means_____ .

   C. To **generate** means _____ .

2. An eclipse of the sun—when the moon passes between the Earth and the sun—is an unusual and interesting **phenomenon** that occurs rarely. Therefore, this occurrence is carefully watched and described by scientists.

   A **phenomenon** is an _____ .

3. Most countries are trying to **reduce** the number of people who cannot read. This problem can be cut down by educating people who live in rural areas.

   To **reduce** means to_____ .

4. People must begin to **moderate** their use of energy. People need to be more reasonable about limiting their use of energy, or the world's supplies will soon disappear. For example, people can work together to save gasoline. They can ride together to work in a carpool. They can **cooperate** by using only one car, not several. People will use less gasoline if they **adapt**, or change their behavior because of a new situation, by carpooling.

   A. To **moderate** means to _____ .

   B. To **cooperate** means to_____ .

   C. To **adapt** means to _____ .

5. Exercise is **beneficial** because a person gets the positive effects of good sleep, straight posture, good health, and reduced appetite.

   Beneficial effects are _____

6. Before the game started, the radio sports announcer studied the strong and weak points of both teams. She was trying to **anticipate** what would happen in the game. Then she used this information to guess at the results. She **predicted** that the state team would win by at least 20 points, and they did. Her **forecast** was correct. What she predicted actually happened.

   A. To **anticipate** means to _____

   B. To **predict** is to _____

   C. A **forecast** is what a person _____

7. Scientists try to understand the world by collecting pieces of information, or **data**, from many places. They then organize the data to see if there are any important relationships among them. They also must think about all the possible influences on the data. These influences are also called **variables**—things that can change or vary depending on the situation. When scientists study all the data and the variables, they are looking for **trends**. These trends may show relationships that indicate changes or general directions of happenings. When they study the data and the variables, they are working with numbers and **statistics**.

   A. **Data** are _____

   B. **Variables** are _____

   C. **Trends** may show _____

   D. **Statistics** are _____

8. Scientists keep records of climate data from many places in the world. They keep records of levels of **precipitation**—that is, the amount of rain, snow, hail, etc. They also keep records of temperature variations and of changes in the **atmosphere**, the air surrounding Earth.

   A. Some types of **precipitation** are _____

   B. The **atmosphere** is _____

9. Not all the information in this report is correct. It should all be **accurate**. **Accuracy** is important in scientific writing because other people depend on the correctness of the information.

    A. To be **accurate** means _____

    B. **Accuracy** is being _____

10. **Fossil fuels** such as coal, oil, and gasoline are burned to provide heat and power for people to live. Fossils are the remains of living things from a different geologic age. They are plants and animals that died thousands of years ago. The remains of the plants and animals turn into coal and oil in the Earth over a long period of time.

    A. **Fossil fuels** provide _____

    B. **Fossil fuels** are _____

Main Reading

The Changing Climate

1   What do fortunetellers and climatologists have in common? Both try to predict the future. Fortunetellers try to "see" people's future lives. They might look at the palms of hands, read cards, or look into a crystal ball. Or they might simply get a feeling about a person and future events. Climatologists try to predict future weather patterns on Earth by studying weather data from the past. They use this information to understand future climate patterns. For climatologists, scientists who study the climate, forecasting weather accurately is a great responsibility. It can save lives and perhaps even the planet.

2   Weather scientists collect and study data from all over the world. They want to understand how weather patterns are changing. In the 20th century, they noticed a slow increase in air temperatures and in the oceans. No one knows exactly why the temperatures are rising. However, scientists believe human

activities cause the warming. They also believe that a warmer Earth will affect people's lives in negative ways. However, the modern way of life requires more and more energy. This energy comes from burning fossil fuels like oil and coal. This is one reason that the Earth's temperatures are getting warmer. The term for this warming is "the greenhouse effect."

3   The greenhouse effect works like this. People burn fossil fuels such as coal and oil for energy. As fossil fuels burn, they release gases. The gases (mostly carbon dioxide, or CO_2) go into the atmosphere, the blanket of air around Earth. CO_2 holds the heat of the sun close to the Earth's surface. The amount of CO_2 is increasing quickly, 31% since 1750. The ozone layer of the atmosphere is also changing because of fossil fuels. Ozone (O_3) forms a protective layer high above the Earth. Like a shield, it blocks heat rays from the sun. Chemicals like chlorofluorocarbons (in refrigerators and hair spray) are changing the ozone that protects the planet. The fluorocarbons are pollutants. They are weakening the ozone layer protection. More heat from the sun reaches the lower atmosphere. And the extra CO_2 holds in the extra heat. Just like a greenhouse, the Earth appears to be getting warmer.

4   Climate data indicate a warming trend. In the 1900s, the average surface temperature increased 0.6 degrees centigrade. The ten years between 1990 and 1999 were the warmest decade since record keeping began in 1891. The warmest year on record was 1998. Data were gathered from tree rings, corals, and glacier ice samples. These data show that the 20th century had the largest temperature increase in the last millennium. One result is the melting of ice. Ten percent of the snow and ice on the Earth's surface has disappeared since 1960. Mountain glaciers are getting smaller. There is more precipitation. The amount of rain, hail, and snow is increasing. It increased by almost 1% each decade in the

20th century. Also, there was an increase in the frequency of storms with heavy precipitation. In fact, there was an increase in clouds over land. There have been fewer extremely cold temperatures since 1950. Warm water masses like the ones caused by the weather phenomenon El Niño and their effects have been more frequent and intense since the 1970s. In the Northern Hemisphere, growing seasons are getting longer. Insects are hatching sooner. Trees are flowering earlier. In addition, sea level has risen between 0.1 and 0.2 meters during the 20th century. The oceans are warmer.

5 Scientists make computer models of climate patterns from weather data. Their computer models are among the most complex in the world. Several variables affect the weather. Therefore, weather models must include many details. Bodies of water and mountain ranges affect the weather. Earth's rotation and the cycle of the moon are weather variables, too. In addition, there are local variables. Forest fires and windstorms must be in the model. So must plant growth and the existence of cities. With these variables in the computer, scientists can determine future weather conditions. Thus, they can predict possible weather situations. They base predictions on weather data from the past.

6 With such models, experts can make useful predictions. They enter possible data into the computer. For example, they can study different amounts of atmosphere carbon dioxide. Fewer cars, for example, produce less CO_2. The model puts all the data together. The computer then gives specific predictions for each amount of CO_2. In this way, experts predict the effects of global warming on climate. There are several hundred atmosphere experts in the Intergovernmental Panel on Climate Change (IPCC). They use computer models to study the effects of global warming. They predict temperature increases around the world of 1.4 to 5.8 degrees centigrade in the next half century.

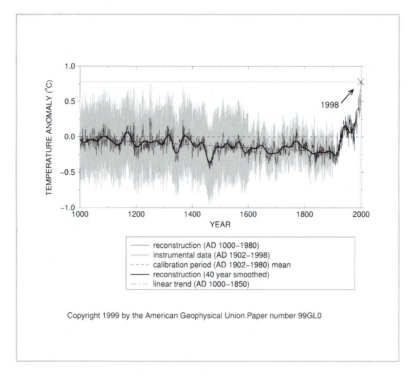

TEMPERATURE ANOMALY (°C)

YEAR

——— reconstruction (AD 1000–1980)
——— instrumental data (AD 1902–1998)
- - - - calibration period (AD 1902–1980) mean
——— reconstruction (40 year smoothed)
- - — linear trend (AD 1000–1850)

7 How will climate change in the future? The answers to this question depend on many different variables. The computer models and the data scientists have collected can be used to generate many possible weather outcomes. All the scenarios, however, include the following effects on people.

8 Negative effects

- lower crop production in most tropical and subtropical regions and some mid latitudes
- less water in many water-scarce regions, particularly in the subtropics
- increased health concerns such as malaria, cholera, and illnesses related to heat
- flooding because of rising sea level and heavy precipitation
- more energy use for cooling because of hotter summer temperatures

9   Beneficial effects

- greater crop production in some regions at certain mid and high latitudes
- increased wood supply because of managed forests
- more water in some water-scarce regions; for example, in parts of Southeast Asia
- reduced winter and cold illnesses in mid and high latitudes
- reduced energy demands for heating because of warmer winter temperatures

10   People will work hard for a long time to adapt to these effects. People must change to survive. In fact, a lot of adapting by people and by natural systems will happen naturally. People will protect themselves and other living things. They will protect endangered animals and plants. People adapt well. Their ability to adapt to climate change depends on technology and education. It also depends on wealth, information, skills, and good management.

11   There are new strategies for managing water, farms, and forests. Water management is particularly important. In semi-dry parts of Africa, for example, digging deep wells for clean drinking water can support many generations. In other areas, farmers are planting new crops. They are changing planting dates. They are raising different farm animals that adapt to new weather patterns. According to the IPCC, improved forest management in the tropics could make a big difference. Trees could absorb 12% to 15% of fossil fuel CO_2. Forest management begins with planting trees. It means saving forests. It means programs to stop deforestation. It means encouraging natural regrowth.

12   Health and urban and rural planning are part of adaptation. Public health planning can include air and water quality, food safety, and surface water management. Better hospitals and clinics must be created. Governments can do a lot. They can teach people about the possible results of global warming. They can

make stricter building laws and plan for land use. And, of course, people can use alternative energy (such as solar and wind energy and fuel cells) rather than fossil fuels.

13   New technologies to limit the use of fossil fuels are developing quickly. There are new wind turbines, for example. There are hybrid-engine cars. The advancement of fuel cell technology and underground carbon dioxide storage could limit the amount of carbon dioxide in the atmosphere. Also, new ways to limit the CO_2 from engines are promising. One goal of scientists is to lower the amount of CO_2 to slow down global warming.

14   These ideas are some ways that people can plan for the future. It is also necessary to find ways to protect natural systems such as glaciers and coral reefs. We must find ways to protect all animal and plant species, forests, polar areas, and wetlands. A changing global climate system is a major concern for the future. International and regional cooperation are essential to meet this new challenge. Preparation, planning, and action are necessary to reduce the effects of global warming on our planet.

Detail Questions: *True* or *False*?

Decide whether each statement is true or false according to the article. Then write the number of the paragraph where you found the answer.

1. Climatologists study weather data to   true   false   _____
   try to predict future climate patterns.

2. CO_2 lets the heat from the sun pass   true   false   _____
   through the Earth's atmosphere and
   into space.

3. There have been more extremely cold   true   false   _____
   temperatures since 1950.

4. The IPCC predicts temperature increases around the world of 1.4 to 5.8 degrees centigrade.　　　true　false　_____

5. One negative effect of a warmer Earth is less water in the subtropics.　　　true　false　_____

6. One beneficial effect is more energy use for cooling because of hotter summer temperatures.　　　true　false　_____

7. One beneficial effect is increased wood supply.　　　true　false　_____

8. Forest management could make a big difference.　　　true　false　_____

9. Using alternative energy is not important in slowing the Earth's warming.　　　true　false　_____

10. People must work to protect natural systems such as glacier and coral reefs.　　　true　false　_____

General Comprehension

Try to answer the questions without looking at the reading.

1. What is the greenhouse effect?

　　_____

2. Why are computer models of climate patterns so complex?

　　_____

3. What is some of the evidence that shows the Earth is getting warmer? List at least five pieces of evidence.

　　_____

4. What is causing the Earth to be warmer? Name three causes.

　　_____

5. What are some ways farmers will adapt to a warmer climate?

   _____

6. What are some ways we can manage forests better?

   _____

7. How can public health planning help?

   _____

8. What are some new technologies to limit the use of fossil fuels?

   _____

Opinions

Here are some ideas from the reading and some ideas about the topic. Read each one and check *I agree, I disagree,* or *I'm not sure.*

1. Human activities are the main reason the Earth is warmer.
   ❑ I agree.　　❑ I disagree.　　❑ I'm not sure.

2. Scientists will never be able to predict the weather accurately.
   ❑ I agree.　　❑ I disagree.　　❑ I'm not sure.

3. People must protect endangered species of animals.
   ❑ I agree.　　❑ I disagree.　　❑ I'm not sure.

4. People need to cut down forests for firewood and agriculture.
   ❑ I agree.　　❑ I disagree.　　❑ I'm not sure.

5. The Earth will continue to get warmer even if people change their habits.
   ❑ I agree.　　❑ I disagree.　　❑ I'm not sure.

Main Ideas

1. The main idea of paragraph 1 is that...

   a. astrologers try to predict the future by looking at stars and planets.

   b. fortunetellers, astrologers, and climatologists all try to predict the future.

   c. scientists are studying weather patterns to predict the future and save lives and the planet.

2. The main idea of paragraph 2 is that...

   a. the Earth is getting warmer because of human activity.

   b. people are burning more and more fossil fuels.

   c. scientists are studying all over the world.

3. The main idea of paragraph 3 is that...

   a. fluorocarbons are weakening the ozone layer's protection.

   b. carbon dioxide holds the heat of the sun close to the Earth's surface.

   c. the process of the greenhouse effect is complex.

4. The main idea of paragraph 4 is that...

   a. the amount of snow and ice on the Earth's surface has decreased by about 10% since 1960.

   b. climate data indicate the world is warming.

   c. trees are flowering earlier.

5. The main idea of paragraph 5 is that...

   a. computer models consider global and local data.

   b. computer models for weather prediction are some of the most complex in the world.

   c. complex computer models use data from the past to predict the future climate.

6. The main idea of paragraph 6 is that...

   a. using computer models enables scientists to make useful predictions.

   b. the computer gives specific predictions for each amount of CO_2.

   c. the IPCC predicts that the average world temperature will increase by between 1.4 and 5.8 degrees centigrade.

7. The main idea of paragraph 7 is that…

   a. computer models and data can be used to generate many weather outcomes.

   b. there will be greater crop production in some regions at certain mid and high latitudes.

   c. people will be affected in both negative and positive ways.

8. The main idea of paragraph 8 is that…

   a. people will work hard to adapt.

   b. people adapt well.

   c. people will protect endangered animals and plants.

9. The main idea of paragraph 9 is that…

   a. farmers are planting new crops.

   b. new strategies for managing water, farms, and forests will be developed.

   c. forest management begins with planting trees.

10. The main idea of paragraph 10 is that…

    a. better hospitals and clinics must be created.

    b. adaptation includes health and urban and rural planning.

    c. governments can do a lot.

11. The main idea of paragraph 11 is that…

    a. new ways to limit the CO_2 from engines are promising.

    b. there are new wind turbines.

    c. new technologies to limit the use of fossil fuels are developing rapidly.

12. The main idea of paragraph 12 is that…

    a. in conclusion, preparation, planning, and action are necessary to reduce the effects of global warming on our planet.

    b. in conclusion, international and regional cooperation are essential to meet this new challenge.

    c. in conclusion, it is necessary to find ways to protect all animal and plant species, forests, polar areas, and wetlands.

 **Related Reading**

Vocabulary Study

Complete the following items and discuss the words with your classmates. Do you use the same or similar words in your language?

Amphibians are animals that usually begin life in the water like fish, but later, as adults, move mostly to land. Using that definition, check (✓) all the following items that are probably amphibians:

_____ frogs   _____ dogs   _____ insects

_____ toads   _____ water birds

A **fungus** is a type of plant that lives off other plants and animals. Using this definition, check (✓) all the following items that are probably fungi:

_____ mold   _____ roses   _____ mildew

_____ corn   _____ mushrooms

To **infect** means to cause to become diseased or sick. Using this definition, which of the following can cause an infection?

_____ virus   _____ germs   _____ fertilizer

_____ fungi   _____ illness   _____ food

What is a hypothesis?

_____

Where Have All the Frogs Gone?

1   According to a group of scientists, 60 to 70 percent of the world population of frogs, toads, and other amphibians has died in the last few decades. Twenty species no longer exist. Biologists have been trying to understand why this is happening. Climate may be the reason. How is this happening?

2   Biologists at Oregon State University have been collecting data on the western toad since the 1980s. These toads live in the nearby Cascade Mountains. Every spring, the toads lay millions of eggs in ponds of water high in the mountains. The eggs usually hatch within one or two weeks. However, by the late 1980s, the biologists noticed that large numbers of the eggs did not hatch. In fact, between 80 and 100 percent of the eggs never hatched. The biologists discovered that a fungus was killing many of the eggs. But they also found that the rays of the sun made the eggs weaker. Because the eggs were weaker, the fungus could attack them. By 1995, the biologists had an idea, a hypothesis, about why this was happening. They thought it was because the ozone layer in the Earth's atmosphere was getting thinner. They believed that more rays from the sun were getting into the atmosphere. The eggs were weakened, so the fungus could infect them.

3   Then the weather changed. Dry years in the late 1980s and early 1990s changed to a few years of greater precipitation in the Cascade Mountains. The water level in ponds in the mountains was much higher. The biologists found that the eggs in deeper water (50 cm) were protected from the sun's rays and did not get infected with the fungus. Eggs in shallow water (10 cm) were weaker because of stronger rays. Forty-five percent of the eggs died in the shallow water from the fungus. The scientists then changed their hypothesis about the cause. Now they blamed climate change, not ozone loss.

4   This study has implications beyond the Cascade Mountains. Weather patterns in the Cascades are connected to large changes in the Pacific Ocean. These mountains tend to get less precipitation during years when the tropical Pacific warms up. This warming causes the El Niño event. The tropical Pacific, generally, has been unusually warm since 1975. This temperature change explains why the population of western toads in the Cascade Mountains

of Oregon has been declining. The unusually warm conditions in the tropical Pacific since 1975 caused dry conditions in the mountains and shallower ponds. The eggs, therefore, were harmed by the sun's rays and vulnerable to fungus infections.

5   This study is an important example of how global climate change affects local interactions. Amphibians all over the world are in decline. Other species are probably in decline as well and need protection for survival.

Source: "Where have all the frogs gone? Studies offer complex reasons why amphibians are vanishing around the world." *The Chronicle of Higher Education.* April 20, 2001. Page A28.

Strategy: Understanding Cause and Effect

Look in paragraphs 2 through 5 for causes and effects of occurrences. Then answer the following items.

Paragraph 2: <u>By the late 1980s, scientists noticed that large numbers of toad eggs in the state of Washington did not hatch.</u> *Why?*

First, or immediate, cause: (fungus)

_____

Secondary cause: (sun's rays)

_____

Third cause: (ozone layer)

_____

First hypothesis:

_____

Paragraph 3: <u>Between 1993 and 1994, more toad eggs hatched.</u> *Why?*

First, or immediate, cause:

_____

Secondary cause:

_____

Third cause:

_____

Revised hypothesis:

_____

Paragraph 4: The population of toads in Washington State has been generally declining since 1975. *Why?*

First, or immediate, cause:

_____

Secondary cause:

_____

Third cause:

_____

Fourth cause:

_____

Paragraph 5: Amphibians all over the world are in decline. *Why?*

Cause and conclusion:

_____

Vocabulary Journal

Choose five words from the Vocabulary in Context list to be your target words. Write the words here:

_____   _____   _____   _____   _____

Now write them in your vocabulary journal. Remember to include the following parts:
- your target word
- the sentence from the Main Reading in which your target word appears
- a definition, including the part of speech
- some sentences of your own

Related Reading

The History of Climate in Tree Rings

1   We think of climate as the unchanging weather patterns of an area. Year after year, the climate stays more or less the same. For example, the climate of much of northern and central Africa is hot and dry. Much of Southeast Asia is hot and wet. Northern Europe has four clear seasons with long winters. The North and South Poles have cold climates. We think of the climate of these regions as never changing. However, there is proof that the climate does change. Tree rings prove it. Each year a tree grows at least a little bit. If there is a lot of rain and a long summer, the tree produces new wood that makes a wide, new light-colored band inside. In cold, dry years, the tree does not grow much. The ring of new wood is a thin, dark line. A piece of a tree will tell the story of the climate while it was living.

2   Some very old trees show that the climate has changed. The bristlecone pine trees that grow in California's White Mountains are some of the oldest living things on Earth. Dendrochronologists, the scientists who figure out the ages of trees from their rings, have found one 4,800-year-old tree. The tree is still living and appears to be healthy. With a special tool, scientists can pull out a thin circular bore. This round stick will show the ring patterns from the outside to the center of the tree. By matching the rings of this tree with the rings of an older dead tree, the scientists have made a record of the climate for the last 9,000 years.

3   Furthermore, there are petrified forests, places where the remains of trees have turned to stone. Scientists can study the rings of these trees, too. They cut across the stone logs. They can study the cross section of a tree that lived many centuries ago.

Thus they know now that climate *does* change. It just takes a long time. Dendrochronology has been an important source of information in the study of climate change.

4   The study of dendrochronology began in 1929 when the first tree-ring scientist, A.E. Douglass, from the University of Arizona, and several other scientists from the Smithsonian Institution and the Museum of Northern Arizona discovered a special old piece of wood. They were working near the town of Show Low, Arizona. They were digging in the ruin of an ancient Indian village. They found an old burned piece of wood among the stones in one of the houses. The scientists studied the tree rings in the old piece of wood. Then Dr. Douglass matched the pattern of the tree rings in the old burned piece of wood with other wood that the scientists were studying. The pattern in the rings in the piece of wood helped the scientists bridge the gap between some even older tree-ring chronology and living trees in the area. Then the scientists could give a date to the time the village had been occupied.

5   When the story about the their discovery reached Europe, the scientists were pleased by the new evidence. The tree rings in the old piece of wood proved that prehistoric people had lived in the southwestern village between the eleventh and thirteenth centuries. This happened before the Norman Conquest of Britain, in 1066 A.D. The study of tree rings and what they tell us about history became important.

6   In fact, dendrochronology became so important that the University of Arizona developed the Laboratory of Tree Ring Research. Scientists from many parts of the world have come to study at the laboratory. These international scientists have come from the People's Republic of China, Russia, Australia, and South America, as well as from other places. The lab work has contributed to the understanding of global change. Scientists have come to the tree-ring lab to learn tree-ring analysis. Then they can work together to solve problems of global change. The workers at the lab have also included archaeologists who study ancient life on Earth. Their knowledge of history contributes to the information scientists need to solve problems in the future. The work of the tree-ring lab adds information about climate changes in the past and possible changes that are taking place now or will in the future.

7   What does the possible change in climate mean to us? Scientists tell us we need to plan for it. Farmers need to develop seeds that can grow in wetter or colder climates. We need to plan for farms in other areas, too. We must also be ready to move— and even to change ourselves. The study of dendrochronology will help people think about their place on Earth.

Detail Questions: *True* or *False*?

Decide whether each sentence is true or false according to the reading. Write the number of the paragraph with the answer.

1. A light-colored tree ring indicates   true   false   _____
    a cold, dry year.

2. Bristlecone pine trees grow in the   true   false   _____
    White Mountains of California.

3. Dendrochronology is the study of   true   false   _____
    petrified forests.

4. People lived in the southwest United   true   false   _____
    States in the 1200s.

5. The climate of Earth is changing.   true   false   _____

Vocabulary Building

1. A **cross section** of a tree is…

    a. a petrified tree.   c. an old piece of wood.

    b. a slice of a log.   d. a light-colored band of wood.

2. A thin **circular bore** of wood is shaped like a…

    a. bandage.   c. bristlecone.

    b. tree ring.   d. a pencil.

3. "They were digging in the **ruin** of a village."
    Ruin means the village…

    a. is nearly new.   c. is large and rich.

    b. was built a few years ago.   d. is no longer there.

4. Tree-ring **chronology** provides scientists with important information.
    Chronology is…

    a. the study of clocks.

    b. the study of petrified forests.

    c. the study of trees and tree-ring patterns.

    d. the study of when events occurred.

5. Their knowledge of history **contributes** to the information that we already have.
    Contributes means that…

    a. knowledge is taken away.   c. history is written.

    b. information changes.   d. knowledge is added.

6. The **analysis** of the problem is the first part of solving it.
    Analysis means the act of…

    a. taking something apart to understand it.

    b. writing something.

    c. working with the answer.

    d. talking about something.

Discussion Ideas

1. Do you think global warming is an important issue for the world? Why or why not?

2. The Earth is getting warmer. How will this fact influence the climate of the place you are from? How will it influence people's lives?

3. Working with a partner, discuss ways that an individual person can help to slow down global warming. Then think about ways a government should respond to this issue.

Writing Ideas

Sometimes a very small change in one area of a large picture can cause a very great change. For example, a change of 1.5 degrees centigrade in a cup of coffee is not much. But the same small change in the temperature of the oceans can affect the weather and climate all over the world.

a. Do some research on the Internet about *chaos theory*. Write an essay about it by first defining it and then using it to explain a weather phenomenon.

b. Do some research on the Internet about climate change. Write an essay about how the climate might be changing in your area of the world.

c. Write about a severe storm or natural disaster—by researching on the Internet or through your own experience, or both. What do you think caused the disaster?

Strategy: Understanding and Writing Clauses

In writing, we often combine ideas and ask questions within sentences. We use verbs such as *say, know, wonder, think, guess, believe, predict, remember,* and *tell* before clauses. Here is an example:

> We want to know why the Earth is getting warmer.
>
> - Why is the Earth getting warmer?
> - What do we want to know?

Note that this example sentence asks a question, but not directly.

1. Here are some more sentences that are related to this unit. Write the two questions in each one. Use your own paper.

   a. Scientists want to know how we can work with rivers to prevent floods.

   b. They need to predict where the storm will be twenty-four hours later.

   c. Scientists understand what causes hurricanes.

   d. They didn't know how they could stop floods.

   e. The scientist told us why there was less rain during the last five years.

2. Now use each of these pairs of questions to make a sentence with a clause.

   a. What did they remember? What did the scientists tell them to do to protect themselves from a hurricane?

   b. What do I believe? What did they say about the negative and positive effects of global warming?

   c. What did the government people wonder? What could they do to help their people?

   d. What do the experts think about? What does the climate information mean?

   e. What did the weather expert guess? What did the strange clouds mean?

3. A clause can also become the subject of a sentence. Here is an example:

   We want to know why El Niño occurs off the coast of South America.

   Why El Niño occurs off the coast of South America is a good question.

Can you form new sentences with the items in part 2 of this exercise? Use the question-word clause in each one as the subject.

Timed Reading 1

What Are Those Lights in the Sky?

In winter, people in the far north see beautiful lights in the night sky. In one out of every three nights, people in Alaska, Canada, Norway, and Siberia see the northern lights. People in some of the northern United States see the beautiful aurora borealis frequently. Even as far south as California and Florida, people occasionally see it. They see the same kind of display in the far Southern Hemisphere. There the southern lights are called the aurora australis.

People who have seen the lights at night have always been interested in them. Eskimo and Tlingit people of North America thought that the aurora was light from the fire of dancing ghosts. Athabaskan people thought that the aurora was light from cooking fires of people farther north. To people in northern Germany, the aurora was light from the shields of angel warriors.

In some places the aurora means bad luck. Some people think that the lights bring disasters. The aurora is strange to people who rarely see it. They believe that the strange lights cause storms and dangerous winds. Actually, scientists tell us that great storms on the sun, called sunspots, cause the lights. These storms cause huge masses of energy particles to leave the sun. These tiny pieces of energy come together near the north and south magnetic poles of the Earth. We see them as lights in the sky. Scientists can predict the northern lights. They watch the sunspots. If there is a storm on the sun, the aurora will appear in a few days.

To the people in ancient Greece and Rome, Aurora was the beautiful and gentle goddess of the dawn (when the sun rises) and mother of the four winds. Boreas was the north wind. Perhaps the people who named the aurora borealis saw the colored lights in the northern sky, moving as if a wind were blowing gently past them. They looked like colored curtains waving in a gentle breeze. They seemed to dance across the northern sky. Truly, the aurora borealis is one of the special beauties of our planet. Have you ever seen the aurora?

Time: _____

Now answer these questions as quickly as you can.

1. People in the far north see the aurora borealis...
   a. more often than other people.
   b. less often than people in California.
   c. about one out of every three nights.

2. People see the aurora as far south as...
   a. California.
   b. Alaska.
   c. Norway.

3. People see the aurora australis...
   a. in Alaska and Canada.
   b. in the far north.
   c. in the far south.

4. The people who thought the aurora was from the fire of dancing ghosts were…

   a. Athabaskan.

   b. Tlingit and Eskimo.

   c. Germanic and Siberian.

5. In northern Germany, people thought that the aurora was from…

   a. the shields of angels.

   b. sunspots.

   c. cooking fires.

6. Some people think that the aurora…

   a. is bad luck.

   b. causes summer and winter.

   c. brings war.

7. Scientists tell us that _____ cause auroras.

   a. cooking fires

   b. sunspots

   c. dangerous winds

8. Sunspots are…

   a. warriors' shields.

   b. storms on the sun.

   c. waving curtains of light.

9. Scientists watch sunspots to…

   a. bring good luck.

   b. predict the aurora.

   c. catch warriors.

10. The main idea of the article is that…

    a. the aurora borealis is named after the dawn.

    b. Boreas was the north wind.

    c. the auroras are special beauties of the natural world.

Timed Reading 2

What Happened to the Dinosaurs?

A long time ago, huge animals called dinosaurs lived on Earth. But they have all disappeared. Scientists wonder about what happened to them. Why did they die? Scientists have been trying to solve this mystery for years. Some scientists say that the dinosaurs died when an asteroid from outer space hit the planet. Now some scientists think that they have the solution, or answer. They have a new hypothesis, a theory.

These scientists say that dinosaurs died because there was not enough oxygen in the atmosphere. The scientists have found tiny bubbles of air in stones called amber. These yellow or brown stones were once the sticky resin—the liquid—inside ancient trees.

Air from long ago is trapped in the bubbles—tiny round spaces inside the stones. Scientists are studying the air in these bubbles. The air in amber bubbles is 35 percent oxygen; air is now 21 percent oxygen. Scientists think that dinosaurs lived between 220 million and 65 million years ago. They lived for a very long time, but slow changes in the atmosphere of Earth made it difficult for the huge dinosaurs to breathe. They needed more oxygen. Their bodies did not change as the atmosphere changed. Therefore, they all died. But why did the atmosphere change? These scientists think that there was a lot of volcanic activity deep inside the Earth. Sometimes hot materials from the volcanic activity came to the surface.

When the volcanoes exploded, the very hot material brought a lot of carbon dioxide (CO_2) into the atmosphere. There was more CO_2 and less oxygen. Therefore, the atmosphere changed. Plants could use CO_2, but animals could not. They needed more oxygen. Because there was not enough oxygen for the enormous dinosaurs and other animals to breathe, they all died. It probably took a long time before all of them were gone—perhaps 10 million years before the last one disappeared.

Scientists call this new theory the Pele hypothesis. (*Pele* is a Hawaiian name for the spirit of the volcanoes on the Hawaiian Islands.) Experts are guessing about what happened, but maybe they are right.

Time: _____

Now answer these questions as quickly as you can.

1. Dinosaurs…
   a. lived a long time ago.
   b. need carbon dioxide.
   c. came from outer space.

2. An asteroid…
   a. is a bubble in amber.
   b. comes from outer space.
   c. is a volcano on Hawaii.

3. A solution is…
   a. a guess.   b. a hypothesis.   c. an answer

4. Amber is…

   a. 21 percent oxygen.

   b. a yellow or brown stone.

   c. used by animals.

5. Resin comes from…

   a. volcanoes.

   b. ancient trees.

   c. dinosaurs.

6. Dinosaurs lived…

   a. 5 million years ago.

   b. in bubbles in amber.

   c. more than 65 million years ago.

7. Some scientists think that dinosaurs died because…

   a. the atmosphere was full of amber.

   b. there was not enough oxygen.

   c. there was not enough carbon dioxide.

8. When volcanoes explode,…

   a. amber is formed.

   b. hot materials come to the surface of the Earth.

   c. the atmosphere gets more oxygen.

9. The last of the dinosaurs died about _____ million years ago.

   a. 5   b. 6   c. 65

10. The main idea of the reading is that…

   a. dinosaurs probably died because of a change in the climate.

   b. amber is a beautiful yellow stone made of the resin of an ancient tree.

   c. dinosaurs needed more oxygen.

THE
COLOR
GREEN

Preparation

Topic

In Navajo, an American Indian language, there is one word for two colors, blue and green. A Navajo speaker can, of course, separate the two colors. There is the blue-green color of the leaves on trees, and then there is the blue-green color of the sky. Can you think of a reason for a language having one word for those two colors? What do you think blue-green means to a person who lives close to nature?

The English word *green* comes from an old English word, *grene*. Two other modern words from this ancient word are *grow* and *grass*. As plants grow, they use water, carbon dioxide, and sunlight to make chlorophyll, the green substance in plants. To many people, green is the color of life. We eat foods that are green. Animals eat green grass and give us milk. Green means health and strength.

Anticipation

Look through the unit. Do the titles of the readings give you clues about the content of the unit? What ideas do you get from the pictures? Why do you think the word *green* is important in this unit?

This list of words contains many natural things. Which of them are (or can be) the color green? Write a check (✓) in front of each one.

_____	tea	_____	rivers	_____	an island
_____	milk	_____	seeds	_____	an ocean
_____	birds	_____	plants	_____	waterfalls
_____	trees	_____	water	_____	mountains
_____	cities	_____	apples	_____	vegetables
_____	lakes	_____	people	_____	golf courses
_____	salad	_____	forests		
_____	grass	_____	tunnels		

Vocabulary in Context

Each of the words in **bold** type is probably a new word to you. Practice with these words and learn more about them.

1. In the western world today, there are two great, important social issues. One is about **human rights**. Should all people have basic human rights such as the right to vote? The other social problem concerns the matter of **respect**. Do people of different cultures and different traditions give rights to people who are different from themselves? Does everyone understand and **appreciate** (or value) the **cultural diversity** of the world?

   A. What are some **human rights**?

      a. money and good houses and nice clothes and cars

      b. music and harmony

      c. the right to vote and to work for a good life

   B. If Person A **respects**, or **has respect for**, Person B, then…

      a. Person A allows Person B to think as he or she wants to.

      b. Person A and Person B are likely to fight.

      c. Person A and Person B always cooperate and think alike.

   C. To **appreciate** is to…

      a. think.

      b. like.

      c. value.

   D. The term **cultural diversity** refers to…

      a. many kinds of people and their values.

      b. a number of important social questions.

      c. the right to vote and the right to fight.

2. Roberto Rodriguez is a young man with a strong interest in the world. He wants to take a **world tour**—alone with his backpack. He spends hours planning his **global** adventure. To learn about the places that a **tourist** can see, Roberto went to several **tourism** offices where governments promote trips to their countries. He has collected a lot of information, and he has **enthusiasm** for visiting those places. He spends hours on-line learning about some **regions** of the world, some general areas or places like the Far East. He went to some travel agencies to get even more information. He is quite excited about his journey. His enthusiasm makes his family wish that he would start his travels.

A. A **global** trip is the same as…

    a. travels.   b. journey.   c. a world tour.

B. A **region** is a place with a name or an _____ .

C. (Use *tour, tourist,* and *tourism.*) A person who **travels** is a

    _____ . He or she is going on a _____ .

    That person is interested in learning through _____ .

D. A person who has **enthusiasm** is _____ about something.

3. Each kind of **wildlife** needs a specific kind of place to live. Some common **habitats** are marshy bogs, coastal areas, and forests. Large numbers of plants and animals live in these places. Marshy bogs, for example, are **ideal** for some kinds of birds. These areas are rich in **biodiversity**. All the conditions for birds are nearly perfect there. Furthermore, a large number of different plants live only in bogs. There is another group of animals that live in forest environments.

A. **Wildlife** refers to…

    a. plants and animals.

    b. people.

    c. trees.

B. A **habitat** is…

    a. a coastal city.

    b. any place to live.

    c. a way of doing things.

C. **Biodiversity** refers to…

    a. the many kinds of plants and animals in a region.

    b. the difference between a plant and an animal.

    c. the different kinds of environments where plants can grow.

D. An **ideal** situation is…

    a. not so good.

    b. good.

    c. perfect.

4. Most of us look like our **ancestors**. Abdul looks like his father, his mother, and his grandfather. His nose is like his father's, but he has his mother's eyes. His ears are small like his mother's ears, but his hair is curly like his father's. He is tall like his grandfather. He has many of the **features** of his family.

   What are some **features** (characteristics) of a person?

   _____

   Who are your **ancestors**? (Give their names, if you can.)

   _____

5. An architect, a person who plans or **designs** buildings, must consider many things. Who will use the building? What kind of heating system is best for the environment? How large must the rooms be? What is the best kind of light for each room? Questions like these will affect the **designs** or plans for the building.

   A. A **design** is most like…

       a. a picture.   b. an idea.   c. a house.

   B. To **design** a building is to…

       a. build it.   b. sell it.   c. plan it.

6. Visitors could see a number of colorful fish in the **shallow** pool in the garden. It was easy for them to see these fish because the water was not deep. In deep water, fish can be **invisible**—nobody can see them.

   A. Something that is **shallow** is not _____ .

   B. No one can _____ something that is **invisible**.

7. A mountain goat watched a mountain climber with a great deal of interest and **attention**. This wild **spectator** saw the woman move around many rough spots. She figured a way to get around many **obstacles** on the mountain. The mountain was a difficult one to climb, but the climber took the **challenge** and made it to the top. The mountain goat ran up the side of the mountain, too, to see where she was going.

   A. Who pays **attention** to something?

      a. someone who is interested in something

      b. every mountain climber

      c. every mountain goat

   B. **Spectators** are people who _____ .

   C. Consider this thought: All **obstacles** are **challenges**, but not all challenges are obstacles.
      Name some **obstacles** for a mountain climber.

      _____

      A hike for one person might be difficult for another person.

      Something that is difficult to do is a _____ for another person.

8. Rain, rivers, snow, and ice have **eroded** the stone of Mont Blanc into the beautiful mountain that it is. These natural forces have formed the cracks and the valleys of the mountain by washing away the rock in some places.

   If water erodes a rock, the rock...

      a. decreases.   b. grows.   c. cracks.

Main Reading

Enjoying the Color Green Somewhere Else

1   The people in the village of Gundrung, Nepal, like to look at the photograph of a nameless young man. The picture is posted on the wall of the village community center. It shows a smiling bearded young man with a backpack, their tourist. The villagers of Gundrung think that he is the best tourist who ever visited their village.

2   What made the villagers so happy about this young tourist? One of the villagers said it best: "He brought most of his own food. He worked with the people to repair (fix) trails near the village. He was concerned about using wood for fuel. He didn't even ask for hot water for a shower." As far as the people of Gundrung are concerned, he was an ideal visitor.

3   In the 1960s, people first became aware of global issues. Many became concerned about global issues like peace, cultural diversity, human rights, biodiversity, and the environment. Even tourists started to think about the people and the surroundings in the regions that they visit. In the past, tourism has often had negative results for local communities. "Taking a trip" meant going to museums and buying souvenirs. Tourists went to enjoy the beaches and see the sights, but they did not interact with the people there. Therefore, these local people saw the visitors only as a source of money. The native people did not respect the tourists, and the tourists did not respect the native people. In fact, the people of the two groups hardly interacted with one another at all—except over money.

4   These tourists visited and enjoyed the surroundings, but they left behind the idea that visitors are people to get money from. Visitors seemed to cause a change in values and traditions. In some cases, because of tourism, the way that the people had always lived actually changed. Their culture changed. The young people see an inaccurate picture of the foreign visitor and then do not want to live in the traditional way. In other words, the tourists went home with happy memories, but the local people and the land are left with problems (such as unhappy young people, and sometimes also drug use and crimes). And sadly, in some cases the land itself, the environment, changed. Although tourism brought lots of money, it also brought damage.

5   A change in the world's awareness, or knowledge about differences in culture, is making a difference in the way people visit other lands. In other words, attitudes seem to be changing. A lot of concerned people have joined organizations to learn more about environmental problems and other populations in the world. These groups began to cooperate with one another and with communities throughout the world. They organized educational groups and friendship tours. And they brought about a new kind of tourism.

6   Lura Shaquielle left her home and stayed in Kenya for two months. When she returned to Manchester, she prepared food for her family in the Kenyan way. She brought home a dress like one that her great-great-grandmother might have worn. She didn't bring home many souvenirs, but she did bring home stories about where her ancestors had once lived. Lura went in search of her "roots" and found a new understanding of her cultural heritage. Her stories about the animals on the broad grassy plains and the thick forests made Kenya real to her family and friends. Lura talked about the dying elephant herds, and the term "endangered species" made more sense to them. Lura talked about the problems with the rhinoceros, and "illegal hunters" took on new meaning. For Lura and her family, being a tourist also has a new meaning.

7   Tourists on trips like Lura's visit communities and lands for new reasons. These travelers are responsible tourists. They want to get acquainted—to get to know the people and enjoy the land—and they act respectfully. Some of the tours are nature tours. People on these tours learn about the environment. They want to see the wildlife—both the animals and the plants in their natural environments. They learn about the land and enjoy its beauty, but they are careful not to destroy anything.

8   By the 1980s, many of the responsible tourists also became environmental tourists. These people traveled not only to enjoy the land and people, but also to help preserve the environment and to work for global peace. Their goal was harmony between all people and the land.

9   The responsible tourists and the environmental tourists became interested in the places they had visited. These people were interested in ecology, caring for the natural state of the environment. They began to look for ways to help conserve (save) the environment, so they joined special tours. At first their fees for the trips helped pay for conservation efforts. The first eco-tours were in Africa and Latin America. There eco-tourists traveled to interesting places and studied the environment. Soon eco-tourists began to organize groups to help in the communities. These groups worked hard; for example, a group of city office workers "got their hands dirty." They built a new trail in an area where rain was eroding the soil on the side of the mountain. They carried stones to strengthen the steep hill and to make steps in some areas. They planted native bushes to hold back the mud in the rainy season. They were ideal eco-tourists.

10   Eco-tourists who return home after such visits can have a great deal of influence. Because of their interest and enthusiasm, they bring some serious problems to the attention of others. For example, because of the efforts (work) of people who care about the environment, some international laws have changed to protect endangered species and to preserve large areas of land.

11   Nowadays eco-tourists can choose from several kinds of tours. They can be "rugged" eco-tourists. Rugged tourists make plans and arrangements themselves. They do not expect comforts like hot water and soft beds. They travel alone or in small groups by foot, train, and bus. Other tourists want adventure, but they also like comfort. These tourists are more likely to travel on organized trips. These trips may include hiking in the mountains, watching birds or whales, digging with archaeologists, sailing on the ocean, or rafting on a wild river. Other eco-tours promote cultural understanding and friendship. Some travelers live with people of the community. All the travel is friendly to the environment and promotes peace and understanding among people of the world.

12   Even the eco-tourist solution to make travel meaningful can create new problems, of course. For example, these tourists were all visiting the same places! In a way, eco-tourists were loving the environment too much. There were too many of them; although they were careful, they were damaging the environment. Someone needed to plan and coordinate travels of the eco-tourists.

13   The travel industry provided solutions. According to the World Travel and Tourism Council, tourism is the world's largest industry. In 1993, $3.5 trillion was spent on tourism. Since the year 2000, a third of all international travelers took some form of nature travel. In 1982 only a few travel companies in the United States planned nature travel; now more than 500 do. Hundreds of travel agencies all over the world offer tours for every kind of tourist.

14   Although the first eco-tourists wanted only to conserve the environment, currently there are few who travel only to look at the natural environment or the wildlife. Like Lura Shaquielle, most tourists want an opportunity to experience a culture different from their own. They want to get to know the people and learn about their way of life. Travel advertisements advertise not only the natural beauty of the environment, but also the people. The ads tell about cultural activities as well as about the wildlife and the natural wonders of the region.

15   The industry of tourism today is founded on principles of respect and cooperation. Tourists now travel to get acquainted with the people and with the land. People in the communities build and maintain hotels and lodges for the tourists. Government officials enforce the laws. When all these groups cooperate, eco-tourism is a benefit to everybody.

Detail Questions: *True* or *False*?

Decide whether each statement is true or false according to the reading. Then write the number of the paragraph where you found the answer.

1. Gundrung is in Kenya.   true   false   _____

2. People of the village of Gundrung liked the   true   false   _____
   young man because he was a good visitor.

3. Before the 1960s, tourists usually visited   true   false   _____
   museums and bought souvenirs.

4. In the past, tourism has left negative results.   true   false   _____

5. Lura visited a village in Nepal.   true   false   _____

6. The first eco-tours were to Africa and   true   false   _____
   Latin America.

7. There are elephants and rhinoceroses   true   false   _____
   in Kenya.

8. Today a third of all travelers will probably   true   false   _____
   take nature tours.

General Comprehension

Try to answer the questions without looking at the reading.

1. What makes a tourist ideal from a Nepali villager's point of view?

   _____

2. What is attractive to tourists about "getting their hands dirty"?

   _____

3. What causes erosion?

   _____

4. What can stop erosion?

   _____

5. What is negative about selling souvenirs?

   _____

Opinions

Here are some ideas from the reading and some ideas about the topic. Read each one and check *I agree, I disagree,* or *I'm not sure.*

1. A single person (such as one tourist) is not a good example of a whole culture.

   ☐ I agree.   ☐ I disagree.   ☐ I'm not sure.

2. Tourists should not buy souvenirs because it shows a lack of respect for the culture of the community.

   ☐ I agree.   ☐ I disagree.   ☐ I'm not sure.

3. In the past, tourists were interested only in pleasure and entertainment, not in the environment.

   ☐ I agree.   ☐ I disagree.   ☐ I'm not sure.

4. A nature tour is a good way to learn about a different culture.

   ☐ I agree.   ☐ I disagree.   ☐ I'm not sure.

5. Travel can promote peace and understanding in the world.

   ☐ I agree.   ☐ I disagree.   ☐ I'm not sure.

Main Ideas

Here are the main ideas for paragraphs 1–5. Write the paragraph number in the blank in front of the main idea of the paragraph.

a. _____ Because of a change in attitude, a new kind of tourism has developed.

b. _____ The visitor worked side by side with the villagers.

c. _____ The negative results of tourism stay with the local community.

d. _____ The young man was a good visitor.

e. _____ Tourists were only a source of money.

Here are the main ideas for paragraphs 6–10. Write the paragraph number in the blank in front of the main idea of the paragraph.

a. _____ Eco-tourists can have a great deal of influence on laws and traditions.

b. _____ Lura learned many lessons while she was a tourist.

c. _____ The goal of environmental tourists is harmony between people and the land.

d. _____ Tourists visit communities and lands for new reasons.

e. _____ Responsible tourists learn something about the land.

Here are the main ideas for paragraphs 11–15. Write the paragraph number in the blank in front of the main idea of the paragraph.

a. _____ Eco-tourists have lots of different choices for their trips.

b. _____ The solution to one problem may create other problems.

c. _____ Nature travel has increased because the travel industry has helped it to grow.

d. _____ Eco-tourists want the opportunity to experience a different culture.

e. _____ Currently tourists travel to get acquainted with people.

Inferences

1. Why do you think eco-tourism is becoming the trendy thing to do?
2. Why do tourists go to distant places to work? (Why don't they work at home?)
3. Why did Lura want to visit Kenya?

Vocabulary Building

1. Eco-tourists are called **responsible** tourists because...

    a. they change the environment.

    b. they live in hotels and like hot water and soft beds.

    c. they show respect to the people and the land.

2. The elephants and rhinoceroses of Kenya are **endangered species**. In other words,...

    a. there are lots of these animals.

    b. people want to keep these animals in zoos.

    c. there are very few of these animals.

3. The tourists built a new trail where rain was **eroding** the soil, and they also carried stones to strengthen the steep hill.

    Which sentence means the same as this sentence?

    a. The rain was washing away the soil, so they built a new trail and carried stones to make the hillside stronger.

    b. They made a new trail because the rain was running down the trail, and they carried stones to make a bridge.

    c. They made a new strong path along the steep hill where the rain was falling gently.

4. To the villagers of Nepal, the young man was an **ideal** tourist. They thought he was...

    a. friendly and nice.

    b. good, nearly perfect.

    c. bad for the village.

5. **Ecology** is most like...

    a. geography.

    b. study of the environment.

    c. elephants.

Vocabulary Journal

Choose five words from the Vocabulary in Context list to be your target words. Write the words here:

_____ _____ _____ _____ _____

Now write them in your vocabulary journal. Remember to include the following parts:
- your target word
- the sentence from the Main Reading in which your target word appears
- a definition, including the part of speech
- some sentences of your own

Related Reading

Rampant Green

1   The name of the plant is kudzu. (It rhymes with "mud zoo.") It is a beautiful rich green color, with large flat leaves. Kudzu, a native plant of Japan, can spread very quickly. This vine (a member of the pea family of plants) spreads because there is nothing to control its growth. It needs only warm air and some moisture. It can take its water out of the air, so it grows even if there is no rain. Kudzu can grow twenty centimeters (one foot) in a single day.

2   Kudzu seems like a friendly plant. It looks beautiful, and its blossoms smell very nice. It covers many dusty pieces of land with rich greenness. Animals like cows and sheep can eat kudzu. In fact, they like it, and they thrive on it. Cows give more milk when they eat kudzu. For farmers who had nothing to feed their livestock, kudzu was welcome. It also stopped erosion, and

it provided good animal food. Furthermore, people can cook and eat kudzu, too. It is nutritious. Kudzu has fibers that can be made into paper and baskets. One can even make syrup and jelly from kudzu blossoms. So this beautiful vine could be a very useful plant.

3   At first farmers were happy to have a plant that grows so easily. Then, however, they realized that kudzu takes over. It grows up the trunks of trees. Then it grows down the tree trunk, twisting itself around the tree. Eventually, the kudzu kills the tree. Another dangerous aspect of kudzu is that it is so strong. In Japan there is an insect that keeps it under control, but not in other parts of the world. There is a chemical poison that can kill it, but that chemical pollutes the groundwater. Furthermore, the poison is extremely expensive. Farmers have tried to dig up the kudzu roots, but one root can weigh over 100 kilograms (220 pounds)! It takes heavy equipment to dig up roots like that. One small root or one seed pod in a truckload of soil can cause another growth of kudzu. This plant is hardy!

4   So far, sheep and goats seem to be the best kudzu control. They eat grass all the way to the roots. With kudzu, the animals don't destroy the wood-like vine stem, but they eat the young leaves and stop the spread of kudzu. Meanwhile, the people who live with kudzu are looking for new ways to use it. Kudzu is cut and baled (like hay). Some people make barn walls from kudzu bales. It's good insulation, they say. Some people burn it, and others make rope. It's easier, they say, to find ways to use the rampant green vine than to stop its growth.

General Comprehension

1. Where is kudzu from?_____

2. There are four ways to control kudzu. What are they?

   _____

3. What are some products from kudzu?

   _____

Inferences

One person wanted to take kudzu seeds to Africa. The land there is dry and dusty. If kudzu could grow there, the people could feed kudzu to their animals. What do you think of this idea? Why is it a good idea? Why is it a dangerous idea?

Related Reading

Golf Green

1   Golf is probably the world's number one participant sport—if it isn't, wait a few minutes and it will be. Making new golf courses is the fastest kind of land development in the world. An average person walks by a golf course and says to herself, "What a lovely place." There is so much beautiful grass, lots of green plants, and pretty ponds. There are birds in the trees and flowers around the clubhouse. The area is quiet, and it seems peaceful. Golf seems like a good thing.

2   This picture of a positive environment, however, is not real. Golf course developers take over good farmland (where people grow food), they destroy the natural habitats of wild animals, and they pollute the water and air. For example, golf course grass

needs a lot of fertilizer and pesticides. The chemical fertilizers seep into the soil and into the water layers between the rocks, the aquifers. Polluted groundwater cannot be used for people to drink. In addition, the air around golf courses has invisible poison gases in it. The fertilizers combine with water to make the grass green—but there are gases that go into the air. The rich grass is also home to many insects. Because these tiny bugs can destroy the beautiful grass, golf course owners put a lot of chemicals on the grass to kill the insects or pests. These chemicals, pesticides, also pollute the water and the air. They kill more than insect pests.

3   The golf courses of the world cover a large part of the Earth. The world's 25,000 golf courses cover an area larger than Belgium. In Thailand, developers build three new golf courses every month. One reason for this growth in the sport is the local community's desire for tourists. Some golfers travel around the world, from course to course. They spend a lot of money, and such tourism brings a lot of money into a country. Golf has become big business.

4   The person who started the game was a ruler, King James. He was from Scotland, where there are small trees, marshy bogs, sand dunes, and grassy areas along the seashore. These coastal areas are called links. King James made up the game of golf for the ordinary people to play. The Scottish links were the course. Hitting the ball around the hills, over the marshes, and through the high grasses was the fun of the game. These natural obstacles made the game challenging.

5   Today most developers do not view the place for a golf course in the same way as King James did. They design golf courses. They change the natural hills, and they make new ones. They add ditches, bushes, and nonnative trees. Golf courses today do not look like the ones that King James played on.

6   Today golf is becoming a spectator sport, too. Like soccer, football, and baseball, many people enjoy watching experts play the game. Only a few years ago, a golf course had long narrow stretches of grass, called fairways. On both sides there was "rough"—land in its natural state. Because more people want to watch golfers, developers have made the fairways wider. In King James's time, no one had to "keep up" the golf links. The land was always natural. Today golfers expect all golf courses to look like parks or gardens.

7   Deforestation is another negative aspect of golf course building. Whole forests of trees are being cut down to make room for the golf courses. After the trees disappear, the land becomes vulnerable to floods. Tree roots go deep into the soil so they can hold the soil in place. The roots of golf course grass are not deep at all; the shallow grassroots are useless against a flood. In addition, forests use a lot of carbon dioxide; all plants need CO_2 for photosynthesis—the food-making process of plants. The grass on a golf course uses a smaller percentage of the CO_2 than trees do. Too much CO_2 causes the greenhouse effect, global warming.

8   Is everything about golf courses bad? No, there are a number of positive sides to the game. Golfers get good exercise, especially if they walk the golf course. A golf course can be environmentally friendly. Some new types of grass are resistant to insects. It is possible to use limited amounts of fertilizer and avoid polluting the groundwater. In a few places, developers are using natural land for golf courses. In an environmentally responsible way, they are using natural hills and marshes for golf courses. Golf does not have to be poison for the environment.

General Comprehension

1. What are three negative aspects of golf courses? How can they be changed to be positive? _____

   _____

2. If King James saw a golf course today, what would surprise him?

   _____

Vocabulary Building

Each of the words in **bold** type is probably a new word to you. Practice with these words and learn more about them.

1. In the reading, **rough** is used in a special way. It means...
   a. fairways.
   b. to keep up the golf courses.
   c. land in its natural state.

2. **Obstacles** are challenges or things that get in one's way. In this reading, obstacles are...
   a. bogs, bugs, and rocks.
   b. hills, marshes, and grasses.
   c. birds, ponds, and rocks.

3. **Invisible** poison gases are gases that...
   a. cannot be seen.
   b. come from the grass.
   c. are seen on golf courses.

4. Natural **habitats** of wild animals are...
   a. golf courses.
   b. farmland that has been changed into golf courses.
   c. places where animals lived before the golf courses.

5. **Deforestation** is a negative aspect of golf course building. What happens?

a. The roots of grasses grow deep into the soil.

b. The grasses use a large percentage of the carbon dioxide.

c. Trees are cut down.

6. After deforestation, the land is **vulnerable** to floods. This sentence means that…

a. the land will use the flood water.

b. a flood can damage the land because it is unprotected.

c. the grasses are useful against the water of the flood.

7. An **environmentally friendly** golf course…

a. helps the environment.

b. pollutes the environment.

c. provides a happy place to play golf.

Related Reading

Beauty

I think that I shall never see
A poem lovely as a tree.

1   When Joyce Kilmer wrote these lines in a poem about trees in 1913, the critics found fault with it. But the readers of poetry loved it. It became the song of the nature-loving public. Kilmer, who died as a soldier in World War I, wrote about trees because he was affected by the beauty of trees. Every tree on Earth—and there are thousands of varieties—is a thing of beauty. One doesn't need to be a scientist to appreciate trees and the many kinds of trees: oak, sycamore, eucalyptus, mangrove, mesquite, cypress, teak,

apple, rubber, maple, or cedar. They are all very different and all beautiful. Furthermore, we have many more reasons to love trees besides their loveliness. In fact, trees are just one of the things about our planet to love.

2   Planet Earth is truly a beautiful place. Nature lovers value the diversity, the variety. It's true: this world of ours is filled with unusual and interesting sites. Most people know about spectacular places like the Himalayan Mountains, the Grand Canyon, Victoria Falls, the Pyramids of Giza in Egypt, Hawaii, the Alps, and Fujiyama (Mount Fuji). In fact, there are places of beauty in every country, in every part of the world.

3   The many varieties of people are a part of the beauty of our planet. The world is made up of people from all races and people of many cultures. The dark-skinned people from parts of Africa and the Middle East, the pale northern Europeans, the small Asian people, and the Native Americans—each group has distinctive features. Each group has a unique kind of beauty. If a person could look at all the members of the human family, what a variety she would see: the young, the old, the tall, and the short; hair in colors of brown, red, gold, silver, white, and black; and eyes in colors from blue and green to nearly dark. In addition, each group of people has a culture all its own, too. To be able to live together in peace and harmony is yet another kind of beauty.

4   The world is alive with colors, too. There's a rainbow of colors in the feathers of birds and in the flowers and leaves of plants. From the deep navy blue of Lake Baikal in Siberia to the azure blue of Crater Lake in Oregon, from the golden white froth of Horseshoe Falls in Niagara Falls, Ontario, to the silver of the Plata River in Argentina, and from the green of the rain forests on Kalimantan (the island of Borneo) to the gem-like quality of green Lake Irazu in Costa Rica, Earth is a colorful, spectacular place.

5   The variety of life forms makes the planet rich in beauty. Biodiversity is beautiful. The oceans and seas are filled with life: the jellyfish floating in the water, the coral reefs, the brightly colored fish, and the dolphins, seals and whales. In the Southern Hemisphere, Australia is home to animals that live no other place on Earth: the kangaroo, the platypus, the fuzzy koala, and the noisy kookaburra in the Australian gum tree. Africa has striped zebras, spotted cheetahs, and bright pink flamingos. In Central America the rain forests are alive with parrots, toucans, and quetzals—birds of many colors.

6   The world is also a place of incredibly wondrous shapes. The frozen waterfall of travertine (stone) at Hamam Meskoutine in Algeria, the turquoise-colored waters of the limestone pools flowing down the mountainside at Pamukkale in Turkey, the white limestone cliffs of Dover, the basalt crystals (another kind of rock) of the Giant's Causeway in Northern Ireland, and the karst dome-rock formations (hills of a kind of limestone) of Kweilin in China—each of them has a unique quality that makes the world a more beautiful place. Even the great open grasslands of the Pampas, the veldt, the steppes, and the great prairies add something to Earth's charm.

7   Each and every person, every animal, every plant, and every geographical feature is part of the great beauty and harmony of Planet Earth.

Strategy: Scanning

This reading contains many names of kinds of things. For example, there is a list of spectacular places: the Himalayan Mountains, Victoria Falls, the Pyramids of Giza in Egypt, the Grand Canyon, and Mount Fuji.

Can you find these words?

1. Words for four kinds of rock in paragraph 6:

   _____ _____

   _____ _____

2. The names of three kinds of birds in paragraph 5:

   _____ _____ _____

3. The names of four great grasslands in paragraph 6:

   _____ _____

   _____ _____

4. The names of three mountains or groups of mountains (mountain ranges) in paragraph 4:

   _____ _____ _____

5. Three specific colors of blue are mentioned in paragraphs 4 and 6. What are they?

   _____ _____ _____

6. Names of Australian animals in paragraph 5:

   _____ _____ _____

7. Names of two waterfalls in paragraphs 2 and 4:

   _____ _____

Vocabulary Building

1. Nature lovers **appreciate** the **loveliness** of trees and flowers. **Appreciate** means to…

   a. notice or see.   b. like and value.   c. find.

   Loveliness means almost the same as…

   a. love.   b. peace.   c. beauty.

2. If a kind of animal is **unique**, then…

   a. it is common.

   b. there is no other like it.

   c. it is truly blue in color.

3. The **diversity** of the world's population is easy to see in cities where people of all **races** live together. **Diversity** means that there are…

   a. two or three kinds.

   b. many varieties.

   c. similar kinds.

   Race refers to people…

   a. with similar features.

   b. from one country.

   c. who are fast.

4. Of the twenty people at the picnic, three found fault with the **site**. These **critics** said that the place was too small, too large, or too public. No one else had any negative things to say.

   Critics are people who…

   a. talk to the public about private things.

   b. like private picnics.

   c. say negative things.

   A **site** is the same as a…

   a. picnic.

   b. place.

   c. critic.

   If a person **finds fault with something**, then he or she…

   a. doesn't see it.

   b. has good things to say about it.

   c. finds negative things about it.

Discussion Ideas

1. "There is no such thing as a citizen of this country or that. We are all citizens of one global village." What do you think? Do you agree? Or do you disagree? Join all your classmates who have the same opinions as you to form a team. List reasons for your opinion. Then (if there are two teams), each team should state one reason, alternating ideas.

2. "Diversity is the spice of life." The quote is a parody or new version of a quote by William Cowper. How does this idea balance the idea of a global village?

3. Use a map or an encyclopedia to look up some of the places or features in this reading. Find pictures if you can. Tell your classmates about the wondrous features of the area that you call home. What do you think is the loveliest site on Earth? What do you think is the loveliest sight on Earth? What makes them beautiful?

4. All the golf courses in the world cover an area the size of Belgium. Kudzu grows over an area two times the size of Lebanon. What do you think of these two important facts?

Organization of Ideas

Statements that support an idea are called the "pros." Statements against an idea are the "cons." Choose one of these scenarios (situation descriptions) and make a list of the pros and the cons.

1. There is a large area of land outside a big city. This land is useless for building because it is too rocky and too wet. However, the land has some lovely ponds and many tall pine trees. A land developer is considering buying the land for a golf course.

2. A village in Zimbabwe near Victoria Falls has been visited by many tourists in the past year. The people in the village are thinking about building a hotel for tourists. They want to build it near the river in the middle of a thick growth of trees.

Writing Ideas

You have just visited Yosemite Park, the Great Pyramids of Giza, Machu Picchu, Niagara Falls, the Great Wall of China, a famous Shinto temple, the Eiffel Tower, the Yukon River, or some other famous, spectacular site. Write a postcard to your best friend about it.

Strategy: Synonyms, Antonyms, and Homonyms

Words that have similar meanings are called *synonyms*. For example, *big* and *large* both mean "great in size." In the following list of words, each word has a synonym. Write the pairs of synonyms on a piece of paper and compare your choices with a classmate's.

tiny	speed	small	enormous
rare	people	cyclone	population
ruin	predict	velocity	countryside
rural	unusual	forecast	
huge	destroy	hurricane	

Antonyms have nearly the opposite meaning. *Large* and *small* are nearly opposite in meaning. Find antonyms for these words within the list and write the pairs of antonyms on a piece of paper. Compare your answers with a classmate's.

rare	cause	result	quickly
rural	urban	slowly	positive
usual	health	sickness	negative

Homonyms are words that sound the same. One pair of homonyms is *here* and *hear*. Write a homonym for each of these words:

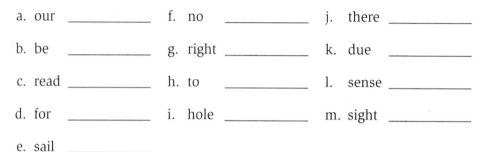

a. our _____   f. no _____   j. there _____

b. be _____   g. right _____   k. due _____

c. read _____   h. to _____   l. sense _____

d. for _____   i. hole _____   m. sight _____

e. sail _____

Timed Reading 1

Biggins Wood

Anna McKane of the *London Observer* said, "They moved heaven and earth to build the Channel Tunnel. They also had to move a forest."

An ancient forest, Biggins Wood, stood in the way of the tunnel entrance under the water between England and France. Because the tunnel goes under the English Channel, people gave it a nickname, the "Chunnel." It is one of the greatest engineering achievements of the twentieth century.

Biggins Wood was rich in biodiversity. For example, it had many beautiful old oak trees. Environmental experts wanted to save the trees for several reasons. One was tradition. There had always been a Biggins Wood. Another reason was sentiment. People loved those trees. The other was a more scientific reason. They wanted to save the genes from the trees: these oak trees were ideal for this environment. For generations of oak trees, they had been growing stronger and stronger. It would be sad to lose them.

Six years before the building of the Channel Tunnel, the forest project began. Students from Wye College collected thousands of acorns from the woods. They planted these oak-tree seeds and produced 2,000 healthy little oak trees. They also collected other small plants of Biggins Wood to plant along with the acorns. They wanted the seedlings to grow within the biodiversity of the first Biggins Wood. Because the soil itself was important, they removed tons of it from Biggins Wood.

This soil was spread over a hectare (2.5 acres). It became the baby-tree field.

The environmental manager of the Eurotunnel Project (its proper name) was in charge of the Chunnel Wood project. Katharine Kershaw, the manager, planned a typical British landscape. She wanted it to look just like the peaceful English countryside. She says that about 220,000 trees and plants are now growing around the tunnel entrance, the railroad, and the side roads. The great oak trees of the area are gone, but not for long. In a few years the new natural growth will merge, joining to make a new Biggins Wood. People leaving the tunnel will see a natural England.

Time: _____

Now answer these questions as quickly as you can.

1. Anna McKane is…
   a. reporter for a British newspaper.
   b. an environmental expert in Biggins Woods.
   c. the manager of the Eurotunnel Project.

2. The Chunnel is the name of…
   a. a college in England.
   b. the tunnel under the English Channel.
   c. the forest that grows near Wye College.

3. One reason to save the oak trees was tradition. In other words,…
   a. people loved the oak trees.
   b. scientists wanted to save the acorns.
   c. there had always been oak trees in Biggins Wood.

4. Another reason to save the oak trees was sentiment. This means that...

    a. people loved the trees.

    b. the trees were ideal for that environment.

    c. people wanted a Biggins Wood.

5. Scientists wanted to save the oak trees because...

    a. the trees were very old.

    b. people liked the trees.

    c. they wanted to save the genes of the old oak trees.

6. The students from Wye College saved...

    a. oak tree seedlings.

    b. the soil from under the trees.

    c. acorns and small plants.

7. The environmental manager of the Biggins Wood Project was...

    a. Anna McKane.

    b. Wye College.

    c. Katharine Kershaw.

8. Katharine Kershaw wanted the area near the English side of the tunnel to look like...

    a. Biggins Wood.

    b. Wye College.

    c. the peaceful countryside.

9. Near the tunnel entrance, there are now ____ trees.

    a. 2.5 million   c. 250,000

    b. 22,000   d. 220,000

10. The main idea of this reading is that...

    a. they destroyed a forest so that they could build a tunnel.

    b. oak trees are important.

    c. modern building projects don't have to destroy nature.

Timed Reading 2

Maligaya Island

Off the coast of Bantangas in the Philippine Islands, there is a tiny island named Maligaya. Its name means "happy." About twenty-five years ago, 100 families lived on this small island. And they were not happy. For half of the year, their island home was dry and yellow; there was too little water to grow much on the island. And their water table was sinking. The other half of the year, there was too much water. Seasonal rains turned the soil into mud. The mud would slide into the ocean, sometimes taking houses with it.

A man named Lino Liquanan lived on Maligaya. He was a veterinarian, a doctor for animals. Lino had a field in front of his office building. He started planting trees there. Every day he spent hours carrying buckets of water to the field. Each tiny seedling got a share of water. On Saturdays, he went to the mainland to get more little trees. The people of Maligaya thought that Dr. Lino was crazy.

The villagers thought Lino was crazy because it was difficult to get the trees to the island. Maligaya does not have a harbor. A person has to wade (walk through the water) in waist-deep water to get to shore. And the sea is dangerous, too, with sea snakes and currents. However, the people of Maligaya respected Dr. Lino and helped him. They saw what he was doing—though they didn't understand his reasons. Lino's field of seedlings grew to a small forest of 40,000 trees.

Lino explained a reason for wanting the trees: they could feed the leaves to their animals. There was so little for animals like cattle to eat on Maligaya that leaves from trees became important as food. Soon every Maligayan family was able to keep one or two cows because of Dr. Lino's trees. For some of the families, the little trees doubled their income.

Over the years the island itself changed. The trees grew, and the people kept planting more. The mudslides and the destruction of houses also stopped. Furthermore, the water table rose two meters!

Time: _____

Now answer these questions as quickly as you can.

1. *Maligaya* means…
   a. "a tiny island."   b. "happy."   c. "yellow."

2. On the island of Maligaya there were…
   a. about 25 families.
   b. about 100 families.
   c. 100 people.

3. The people of Maligaya were not happy because…
   a. they didn't like the yellow color.
   b. they were twenty miles from Bantangas.
   c. their water table was sinking.

4. Lino Liquanan was veterinarian, a doctor for…
   a. people.   b. animals.   c. trees.

5. People thought that Dr. Liquanan was crazy because…

   a. he was wading in the ocean.

   b. he worked in an office building.

   c. he brought trees to the island.

6. To get to Maligaya, Lino had to…

   a. take a boat to the harbor.

   b. wade waist-deep in the ocean.

   c. walk for 25 miles.

7. Lino brought trees to the island…

   a. to use for firewood.

   b. to plant in front of his office.

   c. to build a new office building.

8. Dr. Liquanan's reason for planting trees was…

   a. to provide food for the cattle from the leaves.

   b. to provide firewood.

   c. to build a bridge from the island to the mainland.

9. One result of Dr. Liquanan's hard work was that…

   a. the people waded to the mainland.

   b. every family could have a cow or two.

   c. there were mudslides every year.

10. The main idea of the reading is that…

    a. the solution to one problem may solve others, too.

    b. trees are important to the island of Maligaya.

    c. the water table rose two meters.

TIMED READING CHART

After completing each timed reading, mark your time and comprehension score on the chart. By keeping a written record, you will be able to see the progress you are making. You should try to get your comprehension at 8 or above. Also, notice the number of words per minute you are reading.

- If you are reading below 100 words per minute, you are reading every word very carefully. This speed is good if you need to analyze something in detail.

- If you are reading between 101 and 250 words per minute, you are reading at a speed that is good for studying textbooks and for learning. This is careful reading.

- If you are reading between 251 and 400 words per minute, you are reading at a good speed for casual or informal reading, such as the reading of magazines or newspapers.

- If you are reading above 400 words per minute, you are reading at an accelerated speed. This speed can be used if you need to read something important very quickly. In some cases, this speed actually can help comprehension; it can help you learn information.

Reading Time	Prelim. TR 1	Unit 1 TR 1	Unit 1 TR 2	Unit 2 TR 1	Unit 2 TR 2	Unit 3 TR 1	Unit 3 TR 2	Unit 4 TR 1	Unit 4 TR 2	Unit 5 TR 1	Unit 5 TR 2	Unit 6 TR 1	Unit 6 TR 2	Unit 7 TR 1	Unit 7 TR 2	Unit 8 TR 1	Unit 8 TR 2	Words per Minute
0:00																		
0:10																		
0:20																		700
0:30																		525
0:40																		420
0:50																		350
1:00																		300
1:10																		262
1:20																		233
1:30																		210
1:40																		191
1:50																		175
2:00																		162
2:10																		150
2:20																		140
2:30																		131
2:40																		124
2:50																		117
3:00																		111
3:10																		105
3:20																		100
3:30																		95
3:40																		91
3:50																		88
4:00																		84
4:10																		81
4:20																		78
4:30																		
4:40																		
4:50																		
5:00																		

10   10   10   10   10   10   10   10   10   10   10   10   10   10   10   10   10

Comprehension Ratio

Note: TR = Timed Reading

INDEX

Target and specialized vocabulary items are in italic print. The page numbers provided for each one can be used to locate that item in context. Various topics and activity types are in roman print.